# john shepherd

# youth athletics
## *drills*

Published in 2009 by
A&C Black Publishers Ltd
36 Soho Square
London W1D 3QY
www.acblack.com

ISBN 978 14081 1139 0

A CIP record for this book is available from the British Library.

**Note:** While every effort has been made to ensure that the content of this book is as technically accurate as possible, neither the author nor the publishers can accept responsibility for any injury or loss sustained as a result of the use of this material.

A&C Black uses paper produced with elemental chlorine-free pulp, harvested from managed sustainable forests.

Typeset in 10 on 12pt DIN Regular.

Printed and bound by Martins the Printers Ltd

# CONTENTS

# INTRODUCTION

Athletics can be an incredibly demanding sport, and partly because of this the fun aspect can be lost. Young people don't need to be trained like mini-Olympians; for them, athletics must be fun. Take that away and they are unlikely to return to the track or playing field. It's vital that a track and field coach working with young people is creative and adaptable or they will lose their aspiring young athletes to sports which appear to be more exciting.

For previous generations of children play was a far more physical activity than it is today, despite what the creators of some game station consoles may claim. Health and safety regulations in schools may also have something to do with this decline in physical ability. This all adds up to an increased need for the track and field coach to teach young people fundamental physical skills. Young athletes should learn a repertoire of skills; running, jumping and throwing, that will enable them to be as physically versatile as possible. The ages 8 to 12 have been called the 'skill-hungry' years and it is at this time when fundamental physical skills are most easily learnt.

I aim to show coaches, teachers and interested parents, 101 track and field drills that will feed these skill-hungry years and those that follow – drills that will provide a firm foundation for the performance of all track and field events. Track and field drills are fundamental to all sports. You can't head a football without being able to jump, or bowl a cricket ball without being able to run and throw. This book will therefore be of benefit to coaches from all sports as well as the best one!

# ACKNOWLEDGEMENTS

I have been involved in athletics from the moment I could walk. I recall sprinting to the paper shop in my slippers as a 10- or 11-year-old, to get the papers for my dad (he'd never let me put my trainers on). Not wanting to be seen in the slippers probably unintentionally helped me get fast enough to become an international long jumper a good few years later. Good coaching, however, was certainly more vital and I would like to thank all those that have helped me throughout my career, but in particular Terry Torpey.

I would also like to thank fellow international and track and field coach John Monro for providing comment and advice on this project, particularly with the high jump drills.

This book is dedicated to my uncle Maurice Hughes.

# ATHLETIC DEVELOPMENT AND THE GROWING CHILD

I have taken many coaching sessions with young people and it is crucial to make the activities as much fun as possible (and sometimes be prepared to deviate from your session plan to maintain enthusiasm). Track and field is a technical sport, but a novice is not going to need to learn a two-and-a-half stride hitch kick long jump technique. At this stage the emphasis should be on learning stem skills – skills that will be the foundation for learning more complicated skills at a later age. For the long (and other) jumps providing the young athlete with the basics of how to coordinate their limbs at take-off after a reasonable distance approach run should be the goal.

## Don't just think track and field!

Young people are easily influenced by what they see on TV and in terms of sport, this usually means football! Don't be parochial. I have often tried to coach young people track and field when they would rather be playing football. My advice is to sell them the idea that learning to sprint, jump, accelerate and so on, will make them better footballers; you could let them play football at the end of the athletics session as a reward and to make your point. Who knows you might have the next Christiano Ronaldo (or hopefully Usain Bolt) in your group!

Creativity as a coach is of paramount importance, particularly with the under-11s. Your primary coaching goal is to provide a fun and safe experience and to switch young minds onto a lifelong interest in sport and being healthy.

## Skill windows

There are certain times when a young athlete's body is more susceptible to certain types of training than at others – *see* tables 1 and 2 below. Knowing when these skill windows occur will enable you to select drills and develop workouts that will have the most positive effects on the young athlete. You will also need to be aware of growth spurts in a young athlete's life when they will, for example, be less co-ordinated, due to the way their body is rapidly growing.

For boys the skill window is between the ages of 9 and 12; for girls it is between the ages of 8 and 11.

These skill windows should be seen as the best time to teach the key components of general sports skills – the stems of sports skills. Specialisation in terms of athletic events should be avoided until the mid to late teens. During this learning-to-train phase, the basics of running, jumping, throwing and agility skills can be mastered.

If basic sports skill (physical literacy) is not learned during the young athlete's skill window period, it is unlikely that they will ever reach their full potential.

| Table 1 | Boys – skill windows | | | |
|---|---|---|---|---|
| Age | Skill | Speed | Strength | Endurance |
| 6 | Skill window | | | |
| 7 | Skill window | Speed window 1 | | |
| 8 | Skill window | Speed window 1 | | |
| 9 | Skill window | | | |
| 10 | | | | |
| 11 | | Speed window 2 | | |
| 12 | | Speed window 2 | | |
| 13 | | Speed window 2 | | Aerobic window |
| 14 | | Speed window 2 | | Aerobic window |
| 15 | | | Strength window | Aerobic window |
| 16 | | | Strength window | Aerobic window |
| 17 | | | Strength window | Aerobic window |
| 18 | | | Strength window | Aerobic window |
| 19 | | | | |
| 20 | | | | |
| 21 | | | | |

| Table 2 | Girls – skill windows | | | |
|---|---|---|---|---|
| Age | Skill | Speed | Strength | Endurance |
| 6 | Skill window | | | |
| 7 | Skill window | Speed window 1 | | |
| 8 | Skill window | Speed window 1 | | |
| 9 | Skill window | | | |
| 10 | | | | |
| 11 | | | | |
| 12 | | Speed window 2 | | Aerobic window |
| 13 | | Speed window 2 | Strength window | Aerobic window |
| 14 | | Speed window 2 | Strength window | Aerobic window |
| 15 | | | Strength window | |
| 16 | | | | |
| 17 | | | | |
| 18 | | | | |
| 19 | | | | |
| 20 | | | | |
| 21 | | | | |

# The bigger picture – athlete development

The long-term development of young athletes is vital if they are to be in peak condition in their competitive years. Coaches should use the average ages for peak performance of elite performers in their specific events as a guide to the amount of time that this process can take. For example, throwers often reach their peak in their 30s. Obviously there will be exceptions and some athletes will 'mature' earlier or later. However, you should not rush an athlete and force advanced skills and training loads on them until they are ready.

# Coaching young people

Coaches should not treat children as mini-adults, they should train and talk to them appropriately and most importantly make the training experience as much fun as possible.

'The aim must be to work from success, from things that children can actually do,' says former national athletics coach Tom McNab. Failure to adopt such an approach with young people (and adults) will reduce their self-esteem and may even lead to them dropping out of sport. From a practical coaching standpoint, McNab suggests using coaching practices that allow children to enjoy as they achieve.

## What to say when coaching

To this must be added what is said to the young athlete. Adopting an overly critical approach – even if unintentional – can lead to feelings of low self-esteem. You should therefore endeavour to praise and encourage children through using coaching practices that increase self-esteem.

## Competition, success and failure

Competition can be a contentious area when coaching young athletes. The way competition is introduced can have a crucial effect on their psychology (and future involvement in this and other sports). Athletics is obviously competitive (and many of the drills in this book lend themselves to competition even if this is not the primary aim). Often it will be the 'biggest' – most physically advanced – young athletes who will win, not necessarily those with the most talent. There may be up to five years' physical difference between children of the same age. As indicated, long-term athletic development is crucial. As a coach you must be aware that exposure to defeat at an early age can lead to negative self-esteem and self-belief.

Although a complex area, it is important for coaches to control competition, so that athletes learn to compete, but don't become afraid of doing so because of possible failure, or give up sport altogether because of too many defeats. Where possible, the young athlete should be encouraged to compete against themselves; to record their achievements and better their own performances, rather than trying to beat each other. Achieving a best time or distance will boost confidence.

Reference: *The Coach 20*; Summer 2003; p. 51

# The coaching session

As a coach or teacher working with youngsters who may be thinking about becoming athletes you have a very important role. You are in a position to sow the idea into young people's minds of the benefits of being physically active throughout their lives. This could even lead to a desire to devote much of their lives to training seriously for athletics. To these ends your coaching sessions must be:

- Safe
- Planned
- Targeted
- Progressive and evaluated
- Fun

## Safe

Today health and safety have become major influences on our daily lives. Coaching athletics at all levels is increasingly subject to health and safety policy imposed, for example, by the government, local authorities and UK Athletics (the sport's governing body). Tracks and arenas must be up to standard to host events and training sessions. As a coach it will be your job to ensure that the environment you are coaching in is safe and that the equipment you are using is fit for purpose. You may go to the same venue day after day, but you must always view your coaching set-up with fresh eyes. Don't assume that what was safe yesterday will be so today. Also be mindful of the weather – if it is raining, the track could be slippery and it might be best to avoid activities that require quick turns and jumps (such as agility and throwing).

Ensure that the athletes have the right kit to train in; that you are aware of any medication they may be taking (for example, asthma pumps), and that you or the club or facility you are coaching for have the emergency contact details of everyone you are coaching.

All coaches and teachers and local authority sports workers working with young people should be CRB (Criminal Records Bureau) checked.

## Planned

Plan your coaching session. You should know the age range, general ability levels and the numbers of those you are going to coach. This will allow you to decide what the main aim of your session will be and which warm-up activities to use – some are indicated as more appropriate for the younger (7–11) or older (12–16) age range. In addition, tips are given to make the drills easier or more difficult for different abilities within those age ranges.

You should know what equipment you will need. The drills you select will, of course, determine this. By careful planning the coaching session should be more successful as well as fun.

## Targeted

Targets refer to the outcomes of your session. This should be reflected in your plan. Each coaching session should have a specific outcome. Will the focus be on developing sprint acceleration or will it be on teaching young athletes the basics of the long, high and triple jump take-offs? Select your drills so they are linked. I have grouped them into relevant categories, for example acceleration and reaction drills, arm action drills, cadence drills, and long and triple jump run-up drills. Always select the most appropriate drills for the age group and ability level that you are working with and the specific goals of your coaching sessions. You can pick and choose from the various sections in the book to put your session together, for example, you'll always need to include warm-up drills and you could select sprint acceleration drills, before doing a primarily long jump session.

## Progressive and evaluative

If you want to create better athletes (or fitter young people) then your coaching sessions must be progressive. Each session must be progressive in terms of content, but each must also fit into an overall progressive series of coaching sessions. These should increase the ability and the fitness of the athletes over time.

You will have some athletes who learn very quickly and others who need more time. This is a challenge for the coach or teacher – how to provide a meaningful and enjoyable session for all those involved. If you are working with other coaches you may, after a period of time and analysis, put your athletes into groups. However, this is not streaming – don't make anyone feel less capable than someone else. Always be positive. Making notes after a coaching session will help you (and other coaches) plan and ensure the most positive coaching experience for all those involved.

## Fun

Some conventional athletic coaches may not agree with all the drills I have provided in this book. Many are technical and could be performed by senior internationals, but some are more play orientated. These are included to increase your coaching repertoire and to hopefully make the athletes' coaching experience more enjoyable. Bored people can be difficult to work with – enthused people are not. It is your role as coach to stimulate your athletes and to create a positive learning experience.

# Concerns about training young people

Many people believe that it can be dangerous to train young people – there are fears that the muscular-skeletal system could be damaged, for example. Although this book concerns athletics drills, it is important to point out that any regular, structured physical activity will enhance the physical development of young people.

Finnish researchers looked at the effects of a one-year training programme on male athletes between the ages of 11.6 and 12.6 years. The researchers were particularly concerned with hormonal response.

They found that testosterone (the male growth hormone) concentration increased significantly in the boys. In terms of training adaptation the boys increased speed, power and anaerobic capacity. The control group of non-training boys displayed only slight increases in physical performance over the year. This led the researchers to conclude that 'an increase in anabolic activity with synchronous training ... has positive effects on trainability and physical performance capacity at an early stage in puberty.'

*European Journal of Applied Physiology and Occupational Physiology* 1990; 60(1):32–7.

So, it appears that training young people will not only enhance their physical skills but also their physical development – hence the importance of acknowledging and training according to the skill windows, *see* page 1. The 101 drills in this book will do much to enhance physical skill and develop a young person's physiology.

# Child protection

As coach you have a responsibility to the children in your care. If you are a UK Athletics coach, teacher or youth worker, you will be aware of this and will be subject to police checks and numerous policies and procedures. If a young person discloses information of a personal nature to you, you may have to act. Schools, sports centres and athletics tracks should have an appropriate person/officer to whom you can take your concerns.

# Equipment

Most of the drills described in this book can be performed in any location - sports halls, playing fields and obviously athletics tracks.

The basic items of equipment you will need are:

Bean bags
Canes (preferably multi-coloured)
Cones
Chalk
Tape measure
Stop-watch
Pen and paper
Hoops (preferably multi-coloured)
Whistle
Size 4 and 5 footballs
Quoits
Relay batons
Turbo javelin (these are safe to be used by young people and can be thrown indoors. They come in various weights – 300 g, 400 g, 500 g and 600 g – and different lengths)
Hurdles and foam hurdles
Light medicine balls: 2–4 kg
Jelly balls: 2–4 kg (these can be thrown hard against most surfaces more safely than medicine balls).

Most athletic tracks will have these items of equipment. However, a quick search on the web will soon reveal distributors, or look on the UK Athletics website (www.ukathletics.net).

# The drills

Over the following pages you will find 101 examples of athletics drills grouped by specific categories:

**Warm-up drills** (suitable for all events)
These are grouped into cardiovascular (CV) drills, low to medium intensity preparatory drills and agility drills.

**Running drills**
Includes drills aimed at developing acceleration and reaction, running technique (focusing on leg and arm actions), and leg and arm speed.

**Jumping drills**
These cover the long, triple and high jumps and are concerned with developing a structured consistent run-up and a sound take-off. Some basic 'flight' technique drills are provided.

## Hurdles drills

These focus on developing a sound, rhythmic hurdle clearance technique. Young people can learn to hurdle from any age.

## Throwing drills

These cover the linear and rotational aspects of the throws: shot, javelin and discus.

## Miscellaneous drills

These will enhance athletic performance in its widest sense.

# WARM-UP DRILLS

Whatever the age of the athlete an appropriate warm-up should be completed. The main reason for this is to prepare them physically and mentally for the training session or event which follows. Eight to 11-year-olds are very unlikely to strain muscles, ligaments and tendons, but a 15-year-old might. In adolescence and the years beyond, flexibility levels will decline if they are not challenged by appropriate stretching and active range of movement drills. The increasing muscle mass associated with weight training can also reduce flexibility. Warm-ups should be appropriate for the age group you are working with.

Experience is also crucial: a 15-year-old sprinter who has been training seriously for a number of years is less likely to strain a muscle than a 15-year-old who turns up at the track to do one of your work-outs with a pair of spikes they have never worn before. Be aware and advise accordingly.

## Range of movement and stretching

Range of movement (ROM) is the extent to which a limb or a specific muscle or muscle group can produce movement. Pulling the heel of one leg up towards your bottom whilst standing on one leg will test the range of movement of the main thigh muscle, the quadriceps. ROM is required for the safe and best technical performance of athletic events, drills and skills. The warm-up should be designed to develop specific athletic (and general) ROM.

Until quite recently most athletic warm-ups consisted of a period of light jogging followed by stretches. The latter would usually be 'held', such as bending down to touch the toes, whilst keeping the legs straight, stretching the muscles to the rear of the thighs – the hamstrings. However, research and practise indicates that held stretches are not the best way to warm up muscles for dynamic activity. In fact, for adults these stretches can actually impair the subsequent performance of dynamic activities and cause muscle strains. Today, it is recommended that sports warm-ups involve more dynamic movements that reflect the movement patterns of the sport to be performed. These will develop the sport-specific range of movement required as well as the elastic/dynamic strength needed for the muscles to safely achieve the required movements. Thus the warm-up drills in this section reflect this dynamic approach to warming up. Having said that, dynamic warm-up drills must still be performed with control, with progression and with adherence to form.

## Coaching tip

It is important to keep an eye on children's mobility as their muscles may 'tighten' with age; make sure they can achieve the range of movement required for the drills and of any athletic event they may be training for. At this stage it would be advisable to place a greater emphasis on held stretches to elongate muscles, but these should be performed separately from drills or specific athletic work-outs. A held stretch involves easing into the stretch and holding it there for 10 seconds.

The drills that follow are performed on an athletics track but most can be done in a sports hall, on a sports field or astro-turf. A suggested number of repetitions for each drill is provided, but these are for guidance only. Drills 1 and 2 are warm-up drills with a CV component. Drills 3–16 concern dynamic mobility.

# drill 1  lap jogging (ages 12–16)

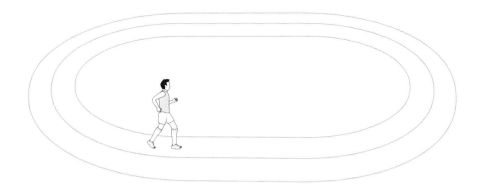

**Objective:** To warm up the heart, lungs and muscles with gentle CV activity to increase viscosity of muscles (making them more stretchy).

**Description:** The athletes jog one or two laps (400–800 m) around the running track.

**Coaching points:** Simply jogging a lap or two is the simplest way to warm up. It's important to stress that the warm-up is not a race!

**Do:** 1–2 laps (or equivalent) depending on the fitness and training maturity of the athletes.

**Variation:** For more experienced athletes introduce gentle sideways, backward, skipping and sprint drills as they jog. This will make the warm-up more fun: jog 20 m, perform a drill, jog another 40 m, perform a further drill and so on. Put one of the more experienced athletes in charge and get them to call out the drills.

# *drill 2* contained warm-up

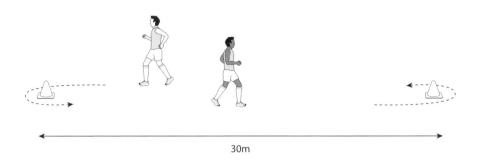

30m

**Objective:** Warm-up (more suited to 7- to 11-year-olds).

**Equipment:** 2 cones.

**Description:** Place 2 cones 30 m apart. The athletes jog up to the first cone, round it and back to the second and round it and so on to complete 6 loops – approx. 360 m (if you have a large group use two or more lanes).

**Coaching points:** Explain that this is not a race and that athletes must stay behind the runner in front of them. Lead the line yourself to ensure the right pace is followed.

**Do:** 6 loops.

**Variation:** Add different elements as for Drill 1. It's important that these should be performed with good technique. Contained warm-ups allow you to watch the athletes and comment and instruct where necessary.

# *drill 3*   overhead ball pass

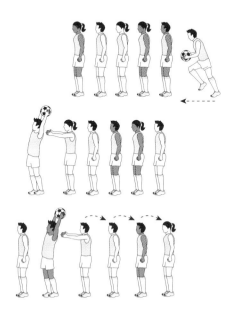

**Objective:** To warm up the trunk and arms to enhance dynamic mobility (more suited to 7- to 11-year-olds).

**Equipment:** Football.

**Description:** Arrange the athletes in straight lines (ideally you'll need 6–10 in each line) using the lanes on the track – it's best to leave a lane (or at least a metre) between each team.

   The athlete at the back of the line runs to the front carrying the football. They pass it over their head to the person behind and so on down the line. The athlete at the end runs to the front of the line and the process starts again. Continue until everyone has run to the front at least once.

**Coaching points:** Athletes must stand tall as they pass the ball.

## Variations:
1   Instead of overhead, change to a sideways turn of the trunk with the ball held in both hands at arms' length to pass ball behind. The next athlete rotates in the other direction to pass the ball behind them.
2   Use a medicine or jelly ball to add resistance.

# ball pass with trunk rotation round circle

**Objective:** To warm up the trunk.

**Equipment:** Football.

**Description:** Form a circle. (A good way to do this is to get the athletes to link hands, with their arms outstretched at shoulder height and then ask them to step back as far as they can without breaking the chain.) Athletes face out and stand with their feet shoulder-width apart. Give the ball to the person at 12 o'clock in the circle. They pass it using two hands to the person to their right who takes the ball at arm's length, rotates and passes it on to the person next to them. Continue until the ball is passed around the circle. Change the direction of the pass once the ball is back to where it started.

**Coaching points:** Encourage rotation of the hips as well as the torso as the ball is passed. Arms should be kept as long as possible.

**Do:** 4 circles to the left and 4 to the right.

**Variations:**
1   Blow a whistle to change the direction of passing at any point during the drill. Speed can also be increased.
2   Use a medicine or jelly ball with older athletes to develop core strength.

# *drill 5* high knee walk

**Objective:** To develop balance, coordination, strength and a feel for the knee lift required when sprinting.

**Description:** The athlete walks forward lifting each leg in turn until their thigh is parallel to the ground. They should coordinate their arms with their legs, bringing their hands in line with their eyes to the front of their body. Elbows should be swung back, behind the body until the upper arm is parallel (or near parallel) to the ground.

**Coaching points:** Encourage an upright posture. There will be a tendency to lean back when lifting the knees to the required height. This can be due to a lack of hip-flexor strength (the muscle at the top front of the thigh). Discourage this. It's better for the athlete to lift their legs to a slightly lower position – they will soon develop the necessary strength and coordination to perform the drill correctly.

With 7- to 11-year-olds you may find that they have difficulty coordinating opposite arm and leg. A fun way to get this across is to show them what they would look like if they walked swinging the same side arm forward in time with the same side leg!

**Do:** 4 repetitions over 15 m.

## drill 6 — high knee lift, with clawing action of lower leg

**Objective:** To further develop optimum sprinting and running technique.

**Description:** Similar to Drill 5 but when lifting each thigh parallel to the ground, the foreleg is pushed forwards and its foot 'swept' down towards the ground in a cycling action. When it contacts the ground the other leg (which should have naturally folded up towards the athlete's bottom) is pulled through to complete its cycle.

**Coaching points:** As with the previous drill encourage an upright posture and opposite arm to leg movement. Explain the drill by saying, 'It's like performing the running action but at walking pace'.

**Do:** 4 repetitions over 15 m.

# drill 7 lunge walk

**Objective:** To develop hip mobility, leg strength and arm–leg coordination.

**Description:** The athletes stand and take a big step forward placing one foot flat on the floor. Their weight is supported on the toes of their other leg and its knee should be close to the ground. From this lunge position they step forward into another lunge as they progress forwards.

**Coaching points:** Encourage an elevated chest and coordination of opposite arm to leg, using a sprint arm action – *see* Drills 45–48.

**Do:** 4 x 6 lunges.

**Variation:** Encourage the 'folding up' of the rear lunge leg (up towards the bottom) as it is pulled forwards into the next lunge (this makes the drill more running specific).

# *drill 8* arm circles

**Objective:** Dynamic warm-up for the shoulders.

**Description:** The athletes stand tall with one arm stretched straight up by their head. Circle this arm back, round, past their head and back to the starting position. Set a number of arm circles to be made and repeat drill with the other arm.

**Coaching points:** Build up speed slowly. The athletes maintain a slight bend at the elbow. They look forwards throughout. Key coaching phrase – 'Brush your ears with your arms'.

**Do:** 4 x 10 repetitions.

**Variations:**
1 Take both arms around at the same time.
2 Change the direction of the swings.
3 Take one arm backward and the other forward (always causes consternation and laughter!).

# *drill 9* leg swings

**Objective:** Dynamic warm-up for the legs.

**Description:** The athletes walk forwards, swinging one leg at a time (with control) to a position in front of their body.

**Coaching points:** It is important that the drill is performed with control, particularly when working with adolescents and novice athletes as their range of movement may be limited (*see* page 9). Under-12s will tend to be more naturally flexible. The torso should remain fairly rigid when the legs are being swung backwards and forwards.

**Do:** 4 x 20 m.

**Variation:** The drill can be performed from standing, using a wall or rail for balance. Doing this allows greater emphasis to be placed on swinging the leg back behind the hips.

# *drill 10* leg cycling

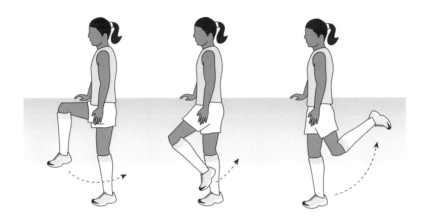

**Objective:** To develop specific running mobility.

**Equipment:** Wall or rail.

**Description:** The athletes stand tall, side on to a wall or rail, placing their inside hand on it for balance. Lift the inside thigh to a position parallel to the ground. Extend the foot away from the body and then sweep it down, round and under, before pulling through to the start position (this completes one leg cycle). Complete a set number of cycles and repeat with the other leg.

**Coaching points:** As with the leg swing (Drill 9) the athletes should resist the temptation to lean back. It is also important to stress the need for a strong torso and not to yield to the movement of the legs. This drill will consequentially develop specific core strength for running, sprinting, jumping and throwing. Note: This strength will take time to develop.

**Do:** 4 x 10 repetitions, both legs.

**Variation:** Increase the speed of the cycling action – advanced athletes only.

# drill 11 'T' stretch

**Objective:** Lower back, hamstrings and hip stretch (also develops core strength).

**Description:** The athletes lie on their back, their bodies forming the 'T' shape. They lift one leg straight up towards their head. At the sticking point (the limit to the athlete's range of movement) they rotate the leg across their body in an attempt to touch the outstretched hand on the opposite side. When their shoulder lifts from the floor, they should pause and then bring the leg back to the centre, before slowly lowering it to the ground. Their other leg should remain pressed into the ground.

**Coaching points:** Some athletes will be able to touch their hands with their feet, others will have more difficulty. Keep an eye on all abilities. Regardless of range of movement the drill should be performed rhythmically and with control.

**Do:** 3 x 10 repetitions to both sides.

# drill 12 lunge with elbow to inside ankle

**Objective:** To warm up and strengthen the hips, hamstrings and bottom muscles.

**Description:** Standing tall the athlete takes a big step forwards into a lunge. They then extend their trunk forwards over their thigh and push the elbow on the same side as the extended foot, down towards its ankle. They pause for a second, and then pull their trunk back to upright before lunging forwards to repeat the exercise.

**Coaching points:** The drill should be performed with control. Younger athletes may lose balance when doing it – with practice they won't!

**Do:** 3–6 repetitions over 10–20 m.

# drill 13 press-up walk (12- to 16-year-olds only)

**Objective:** To warm up the whole body and develop shoulder strength.

**Description:** From standing, the athlete bends forwards placing the palms of their hands on the track, keeping their legs almost straight. They then walk their hands away from them until they are in a press-up position. They will have to bend at the hips to do this (this will stretch the hamstrings and lower back). They then perform a press-up before walking their hands back towards their feet and standing upright.

**Coaching points:** When performing the press-up the whole body should be lowered, not just the chest. As strength is a requirement of this exercise, repetitions should be kept to a minimum. In time strength will develop.

**Do:** 4 x 4 repetitions.

# *drill 14* walking knee lift with 'tug'

**Objective:** To develop balance and hip mobility.

**Description:** Similar to Drill 5 but on each knee lift the athlete reaches forwards with both hands to take hold of their lower leg just beneath the knee. They gently 'tug' the leg to lift it, rising onto their toes as they do so. They then plant the foot on the ground and step forwards with their other leg to perform the drill with the other leg.

**Coaching points:** 7- to 11-year-olds must be instructed to perform the drill with control and to not wrench at their legs! They may also have difficulty balancing – learning to balance is a useful by-product of the drill. Encourage a tall, upright posture.

**Do:** 3 x 20 m.

**Variation:** Perform the drill with eyes closed (advanced athletes only). This will further improve balance.

# drill 15 walking high knee lift with bean bag on head

**Objective:** To develop upright posture, running and core awareness.

**Equipment:** Bean bag.

**Description:** The athlete balances a bean bag on top of their head and walks with a high knee lift, rising on to their toes on each step.

**Coaching points:** Encourage an upright posture as they walk forwards (maintaining the bean bag on their head should assist this). Arms should be coordinated with legs.

**Do:** 3 x 20 m.

**Variations:** Walk faster, play tag.

# *drill 16* side lunge

**Objective:** To develop agility, coordination and leg strength.

**Description:** From standing the athlete takes a big step to one side, then lowers their bottom towards the ground, bending their front leg to about a 90-degree angle. They then step back to the centre to repeat the drill to the other side with the opposite leg.

**Coaching points:** Ensure that the foot of the lunging leg is slightly turned out when placed on the ground. This will allow the knee joint to 'hinge' without strain.

**Do:** 2 x 10 (to the left and right).

# Warm-up drills – event-specific agility drills (medium intensity)

Having completed some of the earlier drills, your athletes should now be ready for more dynamic agility exercises. The following are specific athletics drills – they develop coordination, strength and power that will improve the performance of many of the other drills in this book, and other athletic and sports events.

Agility can be defined as the ability to move swiftly, smoothly and powerfully into dynamic positions.

# *drill 17* backward running

**Objective:** To develop agility, coordination and leg strength.

**Description:** The athlete stands facing backwards to the direction of effort. They run backwards by pushing off from the balls of the feet whilst taking short steps.

**Coaching points:** The athlete should be 'light on their feet'. Arms should be coordinated with legs – opposite arm to leg. When teaching this drill for the first time, stress the need to perform the drill slowly. If you are working with a group set one athlete off at a time. Make sure there are no trip hazards behind the athletes.

**Do:** 4 x 20 m.

**Variation:** Extend (push) the feet further out behind when running backwards to 'open out' the running action.

# *drill 18* sideways skips

**Objective:** To develop agility and coordination and lightness on the feet.

**Description:** The athlete stands sideways on, their feet shoulder-width apart. They bend their knees (to just above 90 degrees) and 'sit back' slightly. Their arms are outstretched at shoulder level and parallel to the ground. The movement is initiated by pushing from the balls of the feet to skip, using a low trajectory sideways.

**Coaching points:** As with backwards running, it is important that the athlete stays light on their feet. Stress the importance of quick, light, dynamic steps – 'left, right, left'. When running, whatever the speed, it is the athlete with the lightest, quickest, most reactive foot contacts that will be the fastest.

**Do:** 4 x 10 m (2 to the left and 2 to the right).

# *drill 19* 'X' steps ('carioca' movement)

**Objective:** To develop agility, coordination and foot speed.

**Description:** The athlete stands sideways on, their feet beyond shoulder-width apart. One leg is taken in front of the line of the body (passing the outside foot) and then immediately pulled behind (what was the outside foot) using very short steps – this creates a crossing movement. The foot movement is repeated to move sideways using this crossing action. Rotate the core and arms in time with the legs, with the arms held approximately parallel to the ground.

**Coaching points:** This drill will tax the grey matter of the young athletes! Go through the drill slowly, step by step, so that they pick up the required movement. In coaching terminology this is called 'chunking'. In time the athletes will be able to put all the chunks together.

**Do:** 4 x 20 m.

**Variation:** Increase the speed of the drill.

**Objective:** To develop agility, coordination and shoulder mobility.

**Description:** The athlete jogs forwards whilst circling their arms forwards.

**Coaching points:** Start slowly then speed up. Encourage an upright posture and making big circles with the arms.

**Do:** 2 x 20 m.

**Variation:** Circle the arms backwards.

# *drill 21* skip with sideways knee movement

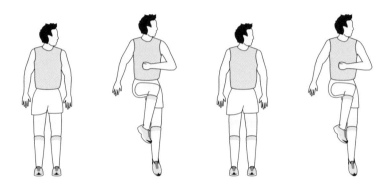

**Objective:** To develop balance, hip mobility and coordination.

**Description:** The athlete skips, taking their knee across their body to waist level and back down as they skip forwards (each skip is made from the same take-off leg). They land on the same leg, step onto their other and back to the take-off leg to skip again.

**Coaching points:** Encourage light feet and a full ankle and leg extension on the skips (take-off). Coordinate arms with legs and keep an upright posture.

**Do:** 4 x 20 m (2 on each leg).

# *drill 22* triangle hop

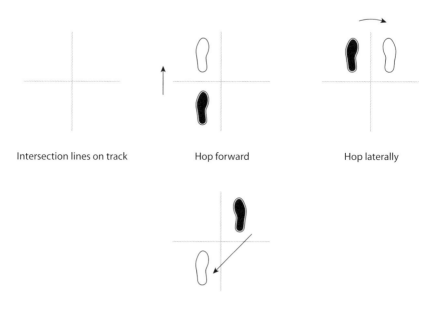

Intersection lines on track      Hop forward      Hop laterally

Hop back to start position

**Objective:** To develop coordination, fast feet, leg reactivity, and knee and ankle strength.

**Equipment:** Tape (depending on location)

**Description:** Mark a small cross on the track or use an intersection of lines on the floor. The athlete hops forwards over the horizontal line and then immediately on to their right foot over the vertical line of the cross and then back to the start position. The hops should be performed with a low trajectory. Athletes hop the points of what would be a right-angled triangle.

**Coaching points:** Stress that light, active ground contacts are crucial. Movements should be made from the balls of the feet.

**Do:** 4 x 10 (2 sets on each leg).

**Variation:** Increase speed.

# drill 23 side-to-side jumps

**Objective:** To develop reactive strength and jumping ability in the legs and ankles.

**Equipment:** Tape (depending on location)

**Description:** Mark a straight line on the ground or use a suitable line on the track. The athlete stands about 40 cm to one side of it and then jumps, using a double-footed jump, sideways over it to land approximately the same distance on the other side. Use a low to medium trajectory. On landing they should immediately react and jump back to the start position.

**Coaching points:** As with the previous drill, reaction with the ground is the key element – it's not about jumping far and high. Stress that the main impetus for the jump should come from the ankle and calf muscles.

**Do:** 3 x 10 repetitions.

**Variation:** Increase speed.

# drill 24 straight leg jumps

**Objective:** To develop lower leg power and agility, and to strengthen the ankle and calf muscles.

**Equipment:** Tape (depending on location)

**Description:** The athlete stands tall, feet shoulder-width apart. They jump into the air primarily using their ankles and calf muscles. Their arms are swung back before take-off, and through and past the hips at the point of take-off to improve jump height and speed.

**Coaching points:** As with the two previous drills, emphasise quick ground contact with the balls of the feet, and a fast reaction. Encourage the athlete to look straight ahead.

**Do:** 3 x 10 jumps.

# *drill 25* line bounce

**Objective:** To develop leg power and fast feet (this drill will develop 'explosive' ground contacts and improve sprint acceleration).

**Equipment:** Tape (depending on location)

**Description:** Mark a line or use a suitable line on the track. The athlete stands approximately 40–60 cm behind it, with their feet slightly wider than shoulder-width apart. They jump across the line using a low trajectory to land on the balls of their feet approximately 40–60 cm on the other side. On landing they should immediately 'bounce' back to the starting position, again landing on the balls of their feet, and react again to jump forwards over the line. This quick-fire drill is repeated for a set number of repetitions.

**Coaching points:** Encourage the use of the arms to help the speed of the drill. Arms should be swung backwards and forwards past the hips to add propulsion to the jumps. Landings must be dynamic.

**Do:** 4 x 10 repetitions.

**Variation:** Time the drill with the athlete counting the number of contacts they make in 20 seconds.

# *drill 26* single leg balance

**Objective:** To develop balance and body awareness.

**Description:** The athlete stands on one leg. They tuck their other leg up towards their bottom and hold this position for a set time.

**Coaching points:** The aim of this drill is to develop balance and awareness of the 'body in space'. Try to get the athletes to relax during the drill and let their natural balance (proprioceptive) mechanisms kick in.

**Do:** 4 x 20 second balances (2 on the left and 2 on the right leg).

## Variations:
1 Perform the balance on tip-toes.
2 Perform the balance with eyes closed.

one-leg ball catch

**Objective:** To develop body control and balance, and to strengthen the legs.

**Equipment:** Footballs, or light medicine or jelly balls for 12- to 16-year-olds.

**Description:** One athlete stands on one leg. Arms should be out in front ready to catch the ball, which will be thrown to them by their partner. The ball should be caught in front of the body. Without dropping their raised foot to the ground, the ball is then thrown back and readiness made for the next throw.

**Coaching points:** Encourage a strong torso. Catching and throwing should be relaxed.

**Do:** 4 x 10 (2 sets of catches and throws on the left leg and 2 on the right).

**Variations:** Introduce a rotational element – get the athlete to take the ball out to one side and behind the line of their hips before they throw the ball back.

# drill 28 agility obstacle course for 8- to 11-year-olds

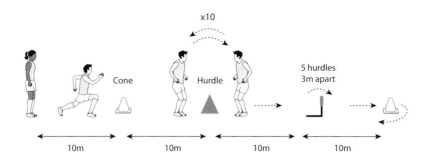

Obstacle courses are a fun way for younger athletes to develop agility and athletic skills – they can form a training session (or lesson) in their own right.

**Objective:** To develop, agility, speed, coordination and balance.

**Equipment:** Low hurdles, cones, hoops.

**Description:** 1) Place a cone 10 m away from the start line. The athletes sprint to this cone. 2) Place a low hurdle (use foam hurdles which topple in both directions) 5 m further on. The athletes have to perform 10 double-footed jumps over the hurdle – this is done by jumping, landing, and turning back to face the hurdle to jump it again. 3) Place 5 low hurdles, evenly spaced (approximately 3 m apart), a further 5 m on. The athletes hurdle these (after landing and sprinting on from the 10th jump of the previous agility challenge). 4) Place a cone a further 10 m on from the last hurdle. After completing this last hurdle the athletes sprint to and round this cone and back to the start.

**Coaching points:** This drill will create lots of excitement for younger athletes. It's therefore best to do it towards the end of your session (or make agility course variations the focus of your work-out), as it may be difficult for them to concentrate afterwards on more exacting skills. The individual components of the course can be practised beforehand.

**Variation:** Put the athletes into teams and perform as a relay.

# RUNNING DRILLS

Running is the foundation of all track and field disciplines. Putting one foot in front of the other at speed seems simple, yet poor running technique will impair performance and could lead to injury, especially in later life. It's also amazing how many people (young and old) don't actually know how to run. The following drills will improve coordination, provide foundation strength and power in athletes' muscles and develop a sound running style.

## Coaching tip

Although the emphasis must always be on fun, you should also look for where improvements can be made. However, you should choose your words and their timing carefully – young people need to be encouraged – they don't want to be constantly stopped and overloaded with lots of technical detail.

## Acceleration and reaction drills

The ability to accelerate is vital for the sprinter, but it is also important for the longer track distances and jumping or throwing events. A middle- or long-distance runner needs to be able to accelerate when fatigued and when making a sprint for the line. Learning to accelerate and move up a couple of gears is therefore crucial. Throwers need to accelerate themselves and whatever they are throwing to optimum velocity at the point of release. Jumpers need to accelerate into and through the point of take-off.

### Reaction time

Reaction (to the starting gun) time is obviously crucial for the sprinter and hurdler and is closely linked to acceleration. Runners of longer distances will also benefit from improved reaction by becoming sharper and 'quicker'. Research with older athletes has found that the fastest 10,000 m runners were also the fastest over 40 m. Similarly jumpers and throwers can also benefit, as the relevant drills will make them more dynamic and powerful. Reaction drills are also fun activities for young athletes.

# drill 29 prone start with 10–20 m sprint

10 - 20m

**Objective:** To develop reaction skills and the acceleration body position.

**Equipment:** Cones to mark finish.

**Description:** The athlete lies face down on the track, their arms by their sides. To a command they get up and sprint the required distance – 10 m is recommended for 7- to 11-year-olds and 20 m for 12- to 16-year-olds.

**Coaching points:** Athletes should focus on using their strongest leg to push themselves up and away from the start line as they move from the prone to upright position. This leg should work 'underneath' their bodies. Older and more experienced athletes should maintain a forward lean for the duration of the sprint and keep low and 'push the track behind them' whilst accelerating.

**Do:** 4–6 starts.

## drill 30 — sitting start, facing against the direction of sprint over 10–20 m

10 - 20m

**Objective:** To develop reaction skills and acceleration.

**Equipment:** Cones.

**Description:** The athletes sit facing away from the direction of the sprint, their palms down by their hips and their legs outstretched. To a command they get up as quickly as possible, turn and sprint the required distance (10 m for 7- to 11-year-olds and 20 m for 12- to 16-year-olds).

**Coaching points:** Tell the athletes which way to turn beforehand (to the right or left) – they should practise in both directions. They all must turn the same way and leave space between each other if working in groups.

As with the previous drill, stress a forward leaning position with the work being done from behind to increase acceleration.

**Do:** 4 repetitions (2 turns to the left and 2 to the right).

# drill 31 running on the spot with 10–20 m sprint

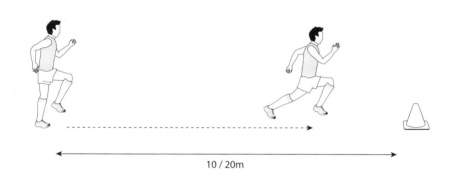

10 / 20m

**Objective:** To develop acceleration and leg speed when accelerating.

**Equipment:** Cones.

**Description:** The athlete runs on the spot, lifting their knees so their thighs are parallel to the ground. Ground contact should be made on the balls of the feet and landings should be light. To a command they sprint the required distance (10 m for 7- to 11-year-olds and 20 m for 12- to 16-year-olds).

**Coaching points:** This drill is great fun and will develop the first driving stride away from the start. Athletes should be forward leaning when they accelerate, driving their arms as fast as possible to assist their acceleration.

**Do:** 4 repetitions.

**Variation:** Increase the running on the spot speed and/or use a low knee lift.

# drill 32 kneeling to sprint 10–20 m

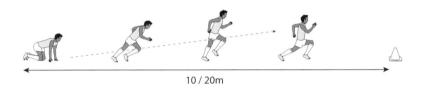

10 / 20m

**Objective:** To develop acceleration.

**Equipment:** Cones.

**Description:** The athlete kneels on all fours. To a command the athlete reacts and sprints from the kneeling position (over 10 m for 7- to 11-year-olds and 20 m for 12- to 16-year-olds).

**Coaching points:** Encourage the first step from the kneeling position to be made with the stronger leg. A low driving position should be maintained.

**Do:** 4 repetitions.

# *drill 33* to the left or right reaction drill

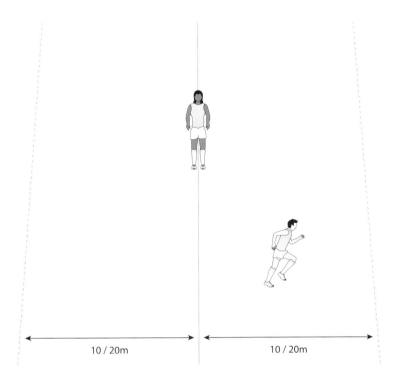

10 / 20m          10 / 20m

**Objective:** A fun way to develop reaction and acceleration.

**Equipment:** Tape/cones.

**Description:** Mark out three lines, each 10–15 m apart or use suitable lines on the track. Line up the athletes along the centre line. They should face you with their legs astride the line. Your command will either be 'left' or 'right'. On hearing this the athletes will turn and sprint in that direction.

**Coaching points:** Although there is a high fun element to this drill, stress the importance of quick pushing strides to accelerate rapidly. Spread the athletes along the centre line.

**Do:** 10 sprints.

**Variations:** Change the commands of 'left' or 'right' to a clap and whistle (having told them which sound indicates left and right).

# drill 34 ball drop reaction drill

**Objective:** To develop reaction and explosive first steps.

**Equipment:** Football.

**Description:** Pair the athletes. One should hold the ball at shoulder height and out to one side of their body; they then drop the ball. The other accelerates and attempts to catch it before it bounces for a second time. Trial and error will be needed to establish the right distance to make the drill most effective.

**Coaching points:** Stress a snappy first step, with a dynamic leg drive. To establish the optimum distance between the athletes, the drill can be performed a number of times starting with a small gap, with the reacting athlete gradually moving further away to the point when they can't quite catch the ball.

**Do:** 4–8 repetitions.

# *drill 35* 'sticky' strides over 10–20 m

**Objective:** To gain a feel for the pushing leg action required for sprint acceleration.

**Equipment:** Cones.

**Description:** From standing the athlete leans forward and then accelerates. As they do so they should emphasise their contact with the ground with each foot, as if the ground is sticky. The idea is to get them thinking about pushing the ground behind them. They should pump their arms to increase their acceleration and maintain a forward lean of the body.

**Coaching points:** Tell the athletes that the ground is made of treacle and they have to push their way over it! If they increase their stride length this should not be discouraged as they need to feel the pushing movement. The push should be made from the balls of the feet. This feeling can be applied to other acceleration drills.

**Do:** 4 repetitions – over 10 m for 7- to 11-year-olds and 20 m for 12- to 16-year-olds.

# drill 36 wall leg drives

**Objective:** To isolate each leg and learn the driving motion required for acceleration (this comes from the hip).

**Equipment:** Wall or suitable height railing.

**Description:** The athlete places their hands flat against the wall to support their body at approximately 45 degrees. Their feet should be shoulder-width apart. From this position, they lift one thigh so that it is parallel to the ground. They then drive it down powerfully, touching the ground with their toes. On contact they immediately pull the leg back to the start position and repeat the movement for a set number of repetitions.

**Coaching points:** Ensure that the athlete's torso is in a braced position and that there is no or little 'hinging' movement at their waist when they drive their leg down and up.

**Do:** 4 x 10 repetition on each leg.

**Variation:** Alternate right, left, right leg drives.

# drill 37 — 'falling' starts over 10 m (12- to 16-year-olds only)

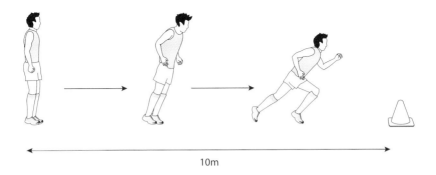

10m

**Objective:** To learn correct leg and body position when accelerating.

**Description:** The athlete stands with feet shoulder-width apart. They then start to lean forwards. When they reach a position where they would fall, they should quickly move one leg dynamically forward to 'catch' their fall and accelerate away.

**Coaching points:** Confidence is required for this drill and it should be progressed slowly. The aim is to achieve a fluid 'fall and sprint' movement. Discourage a 'step and sprint' movement. The athlete's body should 'fall' in a straight position (not bent at the waist). The forward lean should be maintained past the finish line at 10 m.

**Do:** 6 repetitions.

# partner-assisted 'falling' start with 5–10 m acceleration (12- to 16-year-olds only)

5/10m

**Objective:** To develop a low driving position and quick feet required for fast acceleration.

**Description:** Pair the athletes; the one who is going to fall and sprint stands tall. Their partner stands slightly to one side and braces the 'faller' by placing their hands on their shoulders. The accelerating athlete then begins to lean, their weight being taken by their partner. When a 45-degree (or near to) angle is attained the supporting athlete should remove their hands and step to the side, allowing the athlete to 'fall' and sprint 5–10 m.

**Coaching points:** It is important that the athletes take the performance of this drill seriously. Fast, driving steps and a dynamic, pumping arm action are key technical aspects.

**Do:** 4 drills each then swap positions.

# *drill 39* three-point start over 10 m

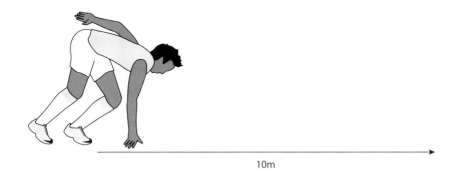

10m

**Objective:** To learn the basics of the sprint start.

**Description:** The athlete places their non-dominant hand on the ground just beyond shoulder width. They make a bridge with their thumb and fingers for support. They bend the dominant knee to do this. Their other hand is taken back with a right angle at the elbow and held high above their shoulder. In doing this they will probably have automatically taken the other leg back behind to gain their balance; if they haven't tell them to do this. The front knee should be approximately 45 degrees to the ground and the other leg flexed slightly at the knee. The athlete supports their weight on the balls of their feet, with their head and back aligned. They will feel slightly uncomfortable (having to control forward movement) in this three-point position. To a command they drive out of the position, keeping low and accelerating as described in the previous drills.

**Coaching points:** If you have included some of the other acceleration drills in your session, the athletes should by now be getting more than an idea of what is required when accelerating fast – remaining low and driving and pumping their arms. If not emphasise these points.

**Do:** 6 repetitions.

# basic sprint start (no blocks) over 10–20 m

10m

**Objective:** To learn the basic sprint start.

**Description:** 'On your marks': The athlete takes two small steps back from the start line and kneels on their weaker knee. They make a fist and place this against the knee of this leg. They position the toes of their stronger leg's foot next to it, tucking the toes under. They should place their hands shoulder-width apart.

'Set position': The athlete raises their hips slightly above their shoulders, whilst moving their weight forwards over the starting line. The position should be slightly uncomfortable.

'Go': The athlete drives away from the start line as fast as possible for 10–20 m.

**Coaching points:** Stress the need to remain low when accelerating from the start position and the need to pump the arms backwards and forwards to add speed.

**Do:** 6–8 repetitions.

# drill 41 'build-ups' (acceleration drill)

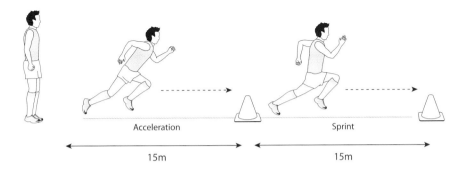

Acceleration

15m

Sprint

15m

**Objective:** To teach the transition from the start, acceleration phase to the more upright sprint phase.

**Equipment:** 2 cones.

**Description:** Place one cone 15 m from the start and the other 15 m beyond in a straight line. Using any of the starting methods already described, the athlete accelerates to the first cone (the drive phase) and then gradually becomes upright to sprint past the second.

**Coaching points:** Emphasise the forward lean of the acceleration phase. Depending on the age and size of the athlete, 15 m may not be long enough for them to execute their 'drive phase' – extend the phase as necessary. Note: the athlete should get into the upright running position gradually (the cones are for reference only and are not to be seen as exact transition points).

**Do:** 4–6 repetitions.

# drill 42 acceleration using markers

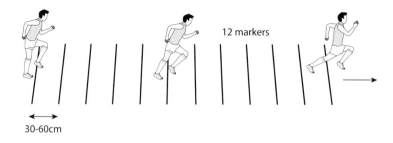

12 markers

30-60cm

**Objective:** Acceleration practice using line markers to develop a gradual increase in stride length with leg speed when accelerating.

**Equipment:** Canes or lines drawn on the running surface (ensure any canes used are not a trip hazard).

**Description:** Position 12 markers at 30–60 cm intervals on the track (these may have to be adjusted for taller and more dynamic athletes). The athlete starts behind the first marker and accelerates, placing one foot at a time through each of the marker gaps with as much leg speed as possible.

**Coaching points:** As with all acceleration practices go for a low driving position with the legs working behind the body. Encourage an 'on the balls of the feet' foot strike.

**Do:** 6 repetitions.

partner catch

Whistle

**Objective:** To develop leg speed in the acceleration phase and reaction.

**Equipment:** Whistle.

**Description:** Pair the athletes. Both start jogging with one starting about 2 m behind the other. To your whistle both athletes start sprinting, with the trailing athlete aiming to pass the one in front. They should sprint for about 20 m or until the whistle is blown again.

**Coaching points:** Make sure there is no risk of collision. At the acceleration signal both athletes should assume a leaning, driving position and push the ground back behind them as dynamically as possible.

**Do:** 6 repetitions alternating positions.

# 20 m sprint to cone from opposite sides

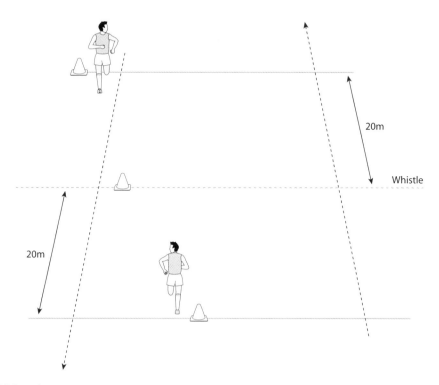

**Objective:** To make learning the acceleration technique a fun competitive exercise.

**Equipment:** Cones.

**Description:** From a cone measure 20 m on either side and position cones at these points. Athlete 1 starts on one side and athlete 2 on the other side facing athlete 1, so they avoid running into each other. Using any of the starting methods described and the command 'on your marks, set and go' the athletes sprint towards each other trying to reach and pass the cone first.

**Coaching points:** Ensure there is sufficient clearance between the cone and athletes when the athletes pass each other. This is still a drill so it is important to provide feedback on the correct mechanics of the athletes' acceleration – under competition this could deteriorate.

**Do:** 4–6 repetitions.

# Running drills to develop fluency, speed and technique

The previous drills have focused on developing reaction, acceleration and correct body alignment when moving from a stationary position. The following drills will develop a relaxed, fluent and technically proficient running technique. If the basics of this are mastered at a young age they will remain with the athlete throughout their athletics career.

Firstly we look at some arm action drills, before moving on to leg drills for improving sprint speed and running technique. The legs supply most of the power for running so they must be strong, powerful and able to move correctly to optimise running speed. These drills will develop key aspects of running technique such as knee pick-up, thigh pull-through (where each leg moves from behind the body to the front) and the drive phase.

# drill 45 running with outstretched arms over 30 m

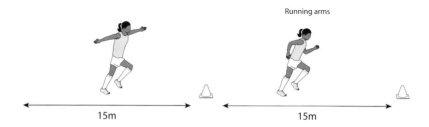

Running arms

15m 15m

**Objective:** To realise the importance of the arms' contribution to running.

**Equipment:** 2 cones.

**Description:** Place one cone 15 m from the start and another 15 m beyond. The athletes run to the first cone holding their arms out parallel to the ground. As they pass the cone they drop their arms and move them in time with their legs.

**Coaching points:** The arms 'drive' the legs when running, particularly at fast and sprint speeds. Many athletes (young or old) don't fully appreciate this. Performing this drill will bring this point home. The arms should remain more or less bent at 90 degrees at the elbow as they are driven backwards and forwards. The hands align with the eyes to the front of the body with the upper arms attaining a position roughly parallel with the ground, behind the body.

**Do:** 4 runs.

**Variation:** Perform the first section of the drill with hands on hips or held straight up overhead.

# drill 46   sprint arm action from lunge

**Objective:** To focus on the sprint arm action by isolating it.

**Description:** The athlete takes a big step forward into a lunge supporting their weight on the flat of the front foot and on the toes of their back foot, keeping their chest elevated, head in alignment with their back and eyes looking forwards. They then pump their arms backwards and forwards as if sprinting.

**Coaching points:** The athlete's hands should align with their eyes to the front of their body and their upper arms should be approximately parallel to the ground behind the body. Shoulders should remain square on to the front and relaxed. The speed of the drill should be increased gradually over a series of repetitions. Relaxation is important as tension will slow the athlete's movements. Hands should be open, with fingers pointing forwards with the thumb resting against their first finger on each hand.

**Do:** 4 x 20 seconds.

**Objective:** To learn the sprint arm action and become aware of the importance of the core (abdominals and back) in this and other athletic movement.

**Description:** The athlete should sit on the track, legs outstretched in front of them, trunk upright. From this position they 'sprint with their arms'. As with the previous drill their hands must reach a position in alignment with their eyes to the front of their body and their upper arm must be approximately parallel to the ground on the back sweep (behind their body).

**Coaching points:** As this drill is performed seated, there will be a greater need for core stability to 'hold' the athlete relatively still. Younger athletes may lack the necessary strength. If this is the case, instruct them to perform the drill at medium speeds – strength will develop over time.

**Do:** 4 x 15 seconds.

partner-assisted sprint arm
action drill

**Objective:** To learn the mechanics of the sprint arm action from a standing position – in particular the back sweep.

**Description:** In pairs, one athlete takes one arm back, maintaining a 90-degree angle at the elbow, so that their upper arm is parallel to the ground. Their partner steps in behind them and places the palm of their same side hand against that elbow. They then position their other palm and arm in the same position to the other side. The first athlete then sprints with their arms, driving their arms back each time to contact their partner's palms with their elbows and bringing their hands to eye level when in front of the body.

**Coaching points:** As with previous drills, shoulders should remain relaxed, the torso upright and held strong to control lateral movement.

**Do:** 4 x 20 seconds.

20 m acceleration into 20 m sprint, emphasising arm drive

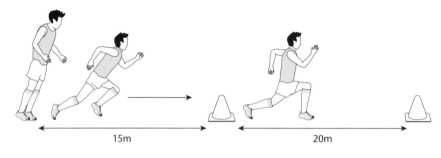

15m      20m

Emphasise arm drive

**Objective:** To put the sprint arm action into 'real' running.

**Equipment:** 2 cones.

**Description:** From a falling start (*see* Drill 37) the athlete runs to the first cone at 90% effort. On reaching the second cone they should pump their arms as vigorously as possible (following the technique as identified in the previous drills) to sprint flat out for the remaining 20 m.

**Coaching points:** Instruct the athletes to 'run with their arms' when they reach the second cone. Look out for signs of poor technique, such as shoulders around the ears or tension in the neck, and correct these. Note: Inexperienced or young athletes will probably not be able to gauge 90% effort. Spend time individually or in small groups going over different speeds. Try using a scale of 1–10 where 1 is standing, 2 small steps, 3 slow walk, 4 fast walk, 5 slow jog, 6 fast jog, 7 slow sprint, 8 medium sprint, 9 relaxed sprint and 10 a flat-out (but still relaxed) sprint.

**Do:** 4 repetitions.

## drill 50 high knee drill

**Objective:** To develop sprint knee lift and correct trunk positioning.

**Description:** Standing, the athlete lifts their knee so their thigh is parallel to the ground, and gradually moves forward. Landings should be made on the ball of their feet. The chest should remain elevated and head held high. Arms must be coordinated with legs.

**Coaching points:** It is important to stress that the knees should move 'away' from the body (angled slightly forwards) and not just be lifted up and down. Doing this will encourage forward momentum. With older athletes, too much high knee work can result in a vertical running impulse and not enough horizontal push. To encourage a tall position throughout the drill, encourage a high hip position.

**Do:** 4 x 15 m.

**Variation:** Increase speed.

# drill 51 heel-to-toe running

The feet are the foundations of the body and their contribution to fast and injury-free running must not be underestimated.

**Objective:** To strengthen the feet and ankles.

**Description:** The athlete takes very short steps using a heel-to-toe movement, knees pushing forward with minimal lift. Arms should be coordinated with their legs, and the chest elevated. They should look straight ahead.

**Coaching points:** Encourage fast, light smooth steps, with powerful arm drive.

**Do:** 4 x 20 m.

**Variation:** If it is a warm dry day and the track is free from debris, the athletes can perform this drill without their trainers. Modern shoes have lots of cushioning designed to protect the wearer from impact forces, but this can restrict the natural movement of the foot and work against developing foot and ankle strength.

# Cadence drills

Leg speed is crucial for sprinters. At elite level a male sprinter will achieve around 5 strides a second. It is important that young athletes maximise their genetic potential by training for speed at the optimum times for physiological adaptation (*see* skill windows page 1). It has been argued that if they do not learn how to maximally 'fire' their legs when young they will not be able to improve on this when they are older. The drills in this section are designed to improve leg speed (cadence).

# *drill 52* bursts

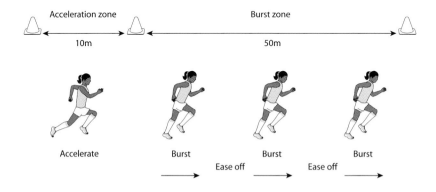

**Objective:** To increase leg speed.

**Equipment:** 3 cones.

**Description:** Place two cones 50 m apart to the side of a lane to mark a 'burst zone', and the third cone 10 m before the first cone to mark an 'acceleration zone'. The athletes use the first 10 m to accelerate into the 'burst zone'. When they enter it, they should try to get in 5–7 bursts of 3–4 very fast strides. They move their legs as fast as possible, slow slightly for a couple of strides and then burst again.

**Coaching points:** Instruct the athletes to accelerate by increasing their leg speed. Tell them not to 'slam on the brakes' when they decelerate, rather they should relax and slow just a little. Relaxation is key and may prove challenging when the athlete is asked to accelerate from an already quick-moving position. Instructing the athletes to use a powerful but relaxed arm drive will help.

**Do:** 4 runs.

# _drill 53_ fast feet ('dabs')

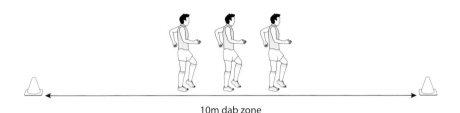

10m dab zone

**Objective:** To develop leg speed.

**Equipment:** 2 cones.

**Description:** Place 2 cones 10 m apart to create the 'dab zone'. The athletes should cover the 10 m distance as fast as they can using very short strides. To do this they must move their feet using very fast up, down and slightly forwards (dabbing) foot movements.

**Coaching points:** Discourage the athletes from looking at their feet – they should look into the distance. Tell them to pump their arms in time with their legs – the faster they move their arms the faster their legs will move. To get the most from this drill they must concentrate – they need to simulate fast body movements mentally.

**Do:** 5 repetitions.

**Variation:** Add a degree of competition with two athletes performing the drill side by side whilst trying to keep up with each other; stress that it is the number of foot strikes that count, not the length of the strides made.

# drill 54 | pull-throughs (single leg cycles) – 12- to 16-year-olds only

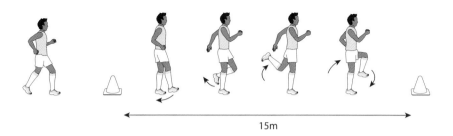

15m

**Objective:** To develop fast strides – specifically the transition from one into the next.

**Equipment:** Cones.

**Description:** Place two cones 15 m apart to the side of a lane. The athlete jogs to the first cone, when they pass it they 'push' one foot forward a short distance in front of their body, using a short, low 'stabbing' trajectory (the foot is not lifted more than a few centimetres from the track and the leg is kept relatively straight). As they do this the other leg is cycled up and behind the body and pulled through to the front and back down to the track as fast as possible. This 'push-cycle' movement is continued until the second cone is reached. Arms should be coordinated with the legs.

**Coaching points:** Once the skill is mastered, some athletes may be able to do two leg cycles to one push, but even a 1:1 ratio requires a very fast cadence and coordination. It is important to stress that whatever the 'cycle ratio', a relatively large range of movement is achieved throughout the drill.

**Do:** 4 (2 on each leg).

# Running – putting it all together

The following drills are designed to increase running speed. They involve the complete performance of the sprint running action. Regular performance of the drills in the previous sections will provide the foundation for enhancing the performance of these drills.

Specifically the bend running drills included address the transition into the straight, which is a crucial aspect of the 200 m sprint.

# drill 55 flying 20 metres

Accelerate — 15m — Flat out — 20m

**Objective:** To develop flat-out speed with relaxation.

**Equipment:** 2 cones.

**Description:** Place a cone 15 m from the start and another 20 m further on. From a falling start (*see* Drill 37) the athlete accelerates so they are near full speed at the first cone. On reaching this point they sprint flat out for the remaining 20 m concentrating on technique.

**Coaching points:** The distances for acceleration and flat-out running will vary between age groups and in terms of acceleration ability and training experience. You may have to vary these distances accordingly. It is crucial that the athlete should be nearly flat out when they hit the first cone and flat out, but relaxed and flowing thereafter. Watch for low hips, tension and a scuttling action in the sprint phase, these are common faults. The sprint action should be rangy, relaxed, balanced and dynamic.

**Do:** 4 repetitions.

# drill 56 fast, relax, fast

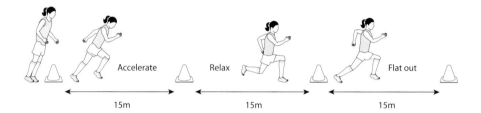

**Objective:** To develop fast leg speed, arm drive and improve sprint speed.

**Equipment:** 4 cones.

**Description:** Four cones should be placed at 15 m intervals by the side of a lane. From a standing start the athlete accelerates hard to the first cone, then relaxes, whilst maintaining speed, before sprinting flat out as they pass the third cone.

**Coaching points:** The athlete must be relaxed as they enter the flat-out phase of the drill. They should concentrate on pumping their arms to increase leg speed and on running tall. Older athletes may need to have the cones placed 20 m apart to get the necessary space in which to best perform the drill. Note: With very young athletes the distance between the cones may need to be reduced.

**Do:** 4 repetitions.

# drill 57 fast, slow, fast, faster! (12- to 16-year-olds only)

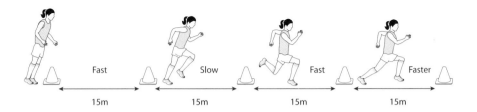

Fast    Slow    Fast    Faster

15m    15m    15m    15m

**Objective:** To encourage greater leg and sprint speed.

**Equipment:** 5 cones.

**Description:** Place the cones at 15 m intervals. The athlete starts from standing by the first cone and accelerates hard to build up speed. On passing the second they slow slightly, before kicking hard as they pass the third cone. Now the difficult bit – they have to try to sprint even faster as they pass the fourth cone.

**Coaching points:** This is a difficult drill for young and inexperienced athletes. The idea of the drill is to develop greater arm and leg speed by the athlete 'firing' their limbs to achieve this from an already flat-out base. A great deal of mental energy will be required. As with the previous drills, it may be necessary to adjust the gaps between the cones so that the drill can be optimally performed.

**Do:** 4 repetitions.

out-of-the-bend run

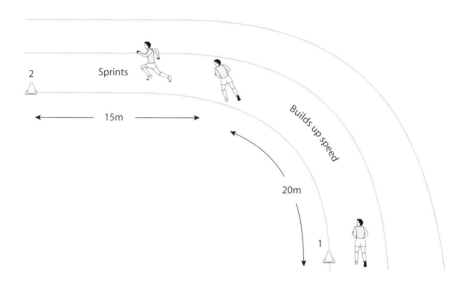

2
Sprints

←——— 15m ———→

Builds up speed

20m

1

**Objective:** To develop bend running skill.

**Equipment:** Cones.

**Description:** Place a cone at the side of one lane, 20 m back from where the bend straightens into the home straight and another cone 15 m into the home straight at the side of the same lane.

From a standing start at the first cone the athlete builds up speed so they are close to top speed as they exit the turn into the straight. They continue to sprint until past the second cone.

**Coaching points:** Bend running is a specific skill. The athlete has to lean into the bend and their body will be subject to considerable torque. Once momentum has built up, the lean into the bend should be made with their whole body and not just the torso. On exiting the bend they should straighten up and focus on running with high hips and relaxation. Ground contacts must be made with the balls of the feet. On the bend the inside foot will twist to control curvilinear forces. An older athlete may need a longer acceleration phase.

**Do:** 4 repetitions.

# drill 59 into-the-bend run

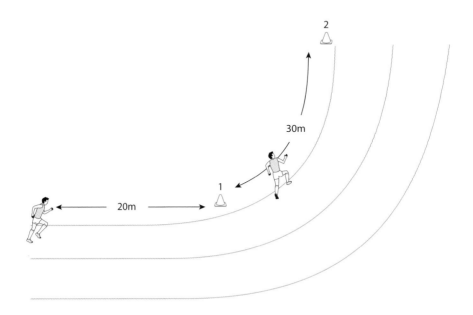

**Objective:** To develop bend running ability.

**Equipment:** Cones.

**Description:** Place a cone 20 m into the start of the bend and another 30 m beyond. The athlete builds up their speed from the start of the bend so that they are at near maximum speed from the first to the second cone. Use any of the starting methods previously described (*see* Drills 29–32).

**Coaching points:** The athlete should lean into the bend (*see* Drill 58). They will experience a different sensation running into the bend compared to the one running out of it.

**Do:** 4 repetitions.

**Variation:** Get the athletes to perform runs from each of the 6 or 8 lanes on the track. Each has a different 'feel' i.e. the inside lanes are tighter. Position the cones at different points around the arc of the bend to experience different sensations.

# JUMPING DRILLS

The long, high and triple jumps are technical events. However, too much time spent on the 'wrong' technical elements will be detrimental to athletic development. It's not worthwhile, for example, trying to teach a hitch-kick (running in the air) long jump technique to an 8-year-old, who has come to the track for some fun. Providing the 'stems' of the jumping skills is more important. As has been noted, young people 'learn' physical skills particularly well between the ages of 7 and 12. If the stems are properly taught at this age athletes will invariably be able to master the more complex athletic skills when they are older. The drills in this section provide the stems for more advanced jumping skills. Note: The pole vault is not specifically covered but many of the drills in this section will be of benefit to this event.

Drills 60–62 are particularly useful for long and triple jump run-up practice, and Drill 63 for high jump run-up practice. Take-off technique drills for long, triple and high jumps follow in Drills 64–71, while Drills 72–77 deal specifically with the triple jump.

# drill 60 establishing an approach run for the long and triple jump

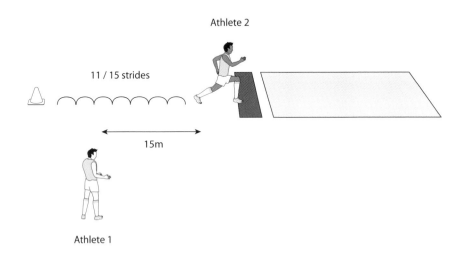

Athlete 2

11 / 15 strides

15m

Athlete 1

**Objective:** To develop a long and triple jump run-up.

**Equipment:** Cones.

**Description:** Pair athletes. One stands about 15 m from the other and to one side of the run-up. The second athlete starts sprinting and their partner counts their strides. They should count 11 strides for the 7–11 age group and 15 for 12- to 16-year-olds. Counting strides could be difficult for the younger age range so you may need to help. (It's easier to count the movement of the leg that makes the first stride, counting 1, 3, 5, 7 and so on.) The first athlete should place a cone marker where their partner's 11th or 15th stride respectively lands. After a full recovery the athlete should start from their run-up marker and run towards the take-off board, attempting to run the same number of strides and get close to the board. They should endeavour to do this without excessive stuttering and stride adjustments. After four attempts the athletes change roles. Each should measure their run-up for future use.

**Coaching points:** Establishing a consistent long or triple jump run-up is difficult. Regular sprint and run-up work will settle stride length over time and lead to consistency.

**Do:** 4–8 repetitions.

# establishing a long jump and triple jump run-up structure

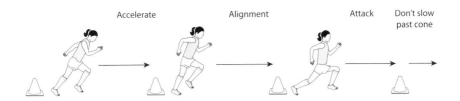

Accelerate    Alignment    Attack   Don't slow past cone

**Objective:** To establish a consistent and balanced run-up.

**Equipment:** 3 cones.

**Description:** The athlete measures out their run-up (*see* Drill 60). Place markers on the side of the lane to divide it into approximately three equidistant lengths. The athlete accelerates to the first cone, then relaxes but continues to build up speed until they reach the second cone, whereupon they attack to – and past – the third cone (which equates to the take-off board).

**Coaching points:** Stress that the markers are for guidance only. Athletes must not be concerned with foot placement, especially near the first and second cones; rather these are cues to 'accelerate', 'align' and 'attack' (to use long and triple jump coaching terminology). More experienced athletes could consider their foot placement near to the third cone, but as with the previous drill it's more about developing run-up consistency and in this case run-up rhythm. Maximum speed is needed at the point of take-off.

**Do:** 6 repetitions.

# drill 62 | long jump run-up and take-off in take-off zone

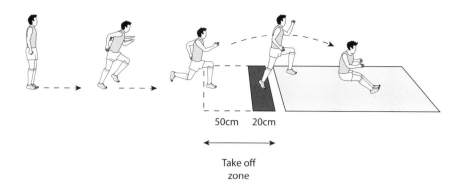

50cm    20cm

Take off zone

**Objective:** To learn how to run up and take off effectively at speed.

**Equipment:** Long jump pit, chalk.

**Description:** Chalk a patch on the run-up 50 cm back from the take-off board – this together with the 20 cm board is the take-off zone. The athlete measures out their run-up (*see* Drills 60 and 61). Using their run-up, they attempt to take off from the take-off zone without dramatically slowing and adjusting their stride pattern. The athlete makes a token long jump (*see* Drill 67) i.e. they do not have to put all their effort into the jump – the emphasis is on the approach and take-off.

**Coaching points:** Encourage relaxation and speed and the 'feel' of the run-up rhythm. Look for upright running (but not leaning back) at 4–6 strides out from the take-off zone. A backward (or forward) lean will have a negative effect on the take-off and jump distance. The athlete should look straight ahead and not for the take-off zone. Note: Do not use this drill for the triple jump unless the athlete is a specialist in this event and over 12, in which case they could perform a hop from the take-off zone and then 'run through' i.e. not complete the step and jump phases of the event.

**Do:** 6 repetitions.

**Variation:** Remove the additional 50 cm take-off zone and get the athlete to take off from the board.

# the curved 'J' approach high jump run-up

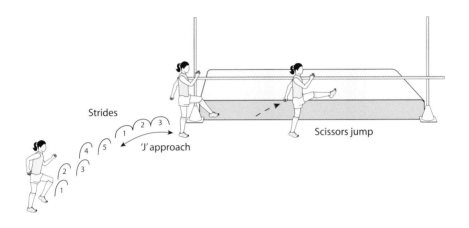

**Objective:** Learning the curved high jump run-up.

**Equipment:** High jump pit (mattress and stands).

**Description:** The athlete runs five strides more or less straight before making a three-stride curved approach to the bar – the 'J'. They make their first stride with their non-take-off foot, so that they take off from their dominant leg. The run-up starts about 1 m outside the nearside upright of the stand, with the take-off being made approximately 70 cm away from the upright. The athlete clears the bar using the scissors technique as described in Drill 68.

**Coaching points:** When running the curve, the athlete should not lean into the bar or towards the mattress. Their take-off foot should be planted at a 45-degree angle to the line of the high jump mattress – this will allow for the knee joint to hinge naturally without risk of injury. Do not use a bar initially so the athlete can focus on the run-up. Use cones to mark both the strides and the path of the 'J' which the athlete follows to run into the bar. The speed of the approach should be moderate and controlled. The athlete should run tall with high hips with foot contacts made from the balls of the feet.

**Do:** 6–10 jumps.

# drill 64 step and take-off for height

**Objective:** To learn the basics of the high jump take-off.

**Description:** The athlete stands tall, feet together, and takes a step forward and then leaps up into the air from their stronger leg – the take-off is made by 'driving' the free (the non-take-off) leg upwards so the thigh is parallel to the ground. The take-off leg is fully extended and the arms coordinated with the legs – opposite arm to leg. The arms can be allowed to continue up and over the head. The take-off ('foot-plant') is made flat-footed.

**Coaching points:** Encourage an elevated chest, head looking forward and a powerful swing of the free leg forward and up, just before and at the point of take-off. The landing should be made on both feet and should be 'soft' – encourage a slight knee yield on landing to achieve this.

**Do:** 10 repetitions.

**Variation:** To add some fun and to attain height hold a football or your hand up just above the high point of the athlete's jump. The athlete attempts to touch the ball or your hand with the top of their head.

# *drill 65* free leg only take-off

This drill can also be used by long, triple and high jump athletes. Regardless of the jumping event it is important that the free leg is driven into the jump; in doing so additional vertical and/or horizontal impetus will be given to the jump.

**Objective:** To be aware of the free leg's contribution to the take-off.

**Description:** The athlete stands on their take-off leg. The toes of their other leg touch the ground lightly just behind their body. They then swing this (free) leg vigorously upwards in order to jump.

**Coaching points:** The free leg is brought through as a 'bent lever'. The athlete tries to maintain a 90-degree angle (or less) at the knee for most of its path as the leg is pulled from behind the body to a position in front of the body. The athlete remains tall throughout the drill. No conscious effort should be made to use the grounded leg to provide impetus to the jump.

**Do:** 6–10 repetitions.

# drill 66 step and take-off for distance

**Objective:** To learn the basics of a long jump take-off.

**Description:** The athlete stands tall and takes a step forward to jump for distance from their take-off leg.

**Coaching points:** As with the previous take-off drills, an elevated chest and dynamic swing of the free leg are required. The athlete swings their free leg forwards and up on take-off. The take-off is performed more quickly than for the high jump (see Drill 64). Less vertical impulse is required in the long jump, which places more demand on take-off speed with a horizontal impetus. Arms must again be coordinated with the legs (that's opposite arm to leg) and the arm action is shorter than that of the high jump with the hand of the forward arm stopping at approximately eye level.

**Do:** 6 repetitions.

three-stride approach long jump

Strides
1  2  3

First stride made with
take-off foot

**Objective:** To develop basic long jump technique from a short run-up.

**Equipment:** Long jump pit and tape measure.

**Description:** From a standing start, taking the first step with their take-off leg, the athlete runs three strides, to take off and jump into the pit.

**Coaching points:** Encourage an elevated chest, head looking forward position and vigorous action of the non-take-off (free) leg at take-off. The free leg should be held during the flight phase for as long as possible before both it and the take-off (now trailing leg) come together and are extended in preparation for landing. Note: Although jumps are measured from the furthest mark back in the sand pit don't worry about the athlete sitting back or making a mark with their hands at this stage. You want to encourage them to get their legs out in front of them on landing.

**Do:** 6 repetitions.

**Variation:** Gradually increase the number of strides taken before the athlete jumps into the pit. More advanced athletes will be able to use their run-up for full long jump practice (*see* Drills 60–61).

# drill 68 — three-stride approach scissors high jump

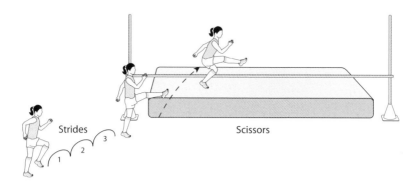

Strides

3

2

1

Scissors

First stride made with take-off foot

**Objective:** To learn the foundations of good high jumping technique. The scissors is old-fashioned, but it is very important for learning the Fosbury technique in the future.

**Equipment:** High jump pit, mattress, stands and bar.

**Description:** The athlete takes three steps from a standing position. A right-footed jumper stands to the left of the high jump mattress – the take-off being made with their right foot which would be to the outside of the mattress. (A left-footed athlete would start from the left.) They aim to take off about 70–100 cm from the mattress, near the upright, so that they clear the bar in the centre, its lowest point. For the right-footed athlete to clear the bar they take their left leg up and over the bar first, with the right leg following. The take-off must be strong and dynamic and made from a flat-footed position. Do not attempt to clear high heights to start with, instead spend time mastering take-off and bar clearance from the short approach.

**Coaching points:** The athlete should go up before they go across. Their inside shoulder must not lean into the bar.

**Do:** 6–10 jumps.

**Variation:** Perform the jump from 8 strides using the 'J' approach – *see* Drill 63.

Accelerate

3 strides  3 strides  3 strides

**Objective:** To develop a consistent long jump take-off and spatial awareness.

**Equipment:** 4–6 low foam hurdles.

**Description:** Place the hurdles equidistant in a straight line on the running track. The gap between each will depend on the age of the athlete and their ability. The athlete must be able to run 3 strides between each. From a standing start the athlete runs at medium speed and clears the first hurdle using a long jump take-off action (from their strongest leg). They should land on their non-take-off leg, step forward and run 3 strides to perform another take-off over the next hurdle – this process is repeated until all the hurdles are cleared.

**Coaching points:** Encourage the athlete to keep their trunk elevated at take-off and look straight ahead. The take-off should be dynamic, active and result in forward (and upward) propulsion. More specifically, you're looking for a full extension of the take-off leg as the athlete leaves the ground and the holding of the free leg at thigh level, parallel to the ground, for a split second after take-off.

**Do:** 6 repetitions.

# *drill 70* alternate leg take-offs ('skips')

Right                                    Left

**Objective:** To develop general jumping and take-off ability.

**Description:** From standing the athlete skips forward performing a type of long jump take-off but with a greater vertical element (they go up and forwards). They land on their take-off foot and immediately perform another jump from their other leg – this is achieved by dropping their free leg to the ground (it should have been at thigh level parallel to the ground in the first jump) and jumping from it to lift into another jump. The first take-off action is reversed on each jump.

**Coaching points:** Stress that landings need to be 'active'. Advanced athletes could be instructed to pull the take-off foot back rapidly towards the track surface the split second before they leap into each jump. The chest should remain elevated, with the arms coordinated with legs and the athlete should look straight ahead.

**Do:** 6 repetitions – over 10 or 20 m depending on the experience of the athletes.

# drill 71 standing long jump

**Objective:** To introduce the long jump leg shoot (and to develop leg power).

**Equipment:** Long jump pit, tape measure.

**Description:** The athlete stands at the edge of the long jump pit. They bend their knees and swing their arms backwards and forwards. When ready they extend their legs and jump as far as they can forwards into the pit. At the point of take-off their arms should be swinging past their hips to transfer power into the jump.

**Coaching points:** Encourage the athlete to look as far into the distance as possible when they jump (and not down) – this will prevent the head from affecting their trajectory. Also encourage them to get their legs out in front when landing. Although this may result in them sitting back into the pit, they will begin to get used to the idea of developing a leg shoot (legs extended landing position), which will transfer into actual long jumping.

**Do:** 6 repetitions.

# Triple jump

The triple jump is a complex but fun event. In just a few sessions young athletes will improve dramatically. It is a taxing event on the legs and coaches must take care not to do too much intense work. Having said that, jumping is a natural play activity for children and it is only when serious training and conditioning starts that real control needs to be exerted on the intensity of training sessions. The drills in this section are designed to introduce the event and to master the three phases – the hop, the step and the jump.

triple jump – the hop

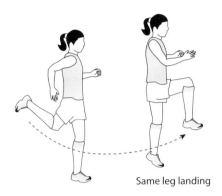

Same leg landing

**Objective:** Learning the hop phase (also develops leg power).

**Description:** The athlete stands on one leg and then hops, their non-hopping leg should be folded behind them. This is swung through in time with the take-off leg to boost hop power.

**Coaching points:** Many athletes will find hopping relatively difficult. They should keep their chest elevated and be as tall as possible during the movement. They should practise on both legs and identify which is their stronger as this is generally used to perform both the hop and step phases of the triple jump (and the long and high jump take-offs). Encourage the cycling of the non-hopping leg underneath their bodies and round off to a position in front. Note: It may take time for the athlete to develop the strength and power required. Landings must be soft with the knee slightly flexed.

**Do:** 6–10 hops on both legs.

**Variation:** Perform the hop with a short 3- or 5-stride run-up.

# drill 73 multiple hops

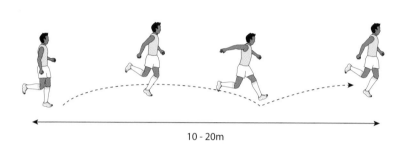

10 - 20m

**Objective:** To master triple jump hopping at speed (also develops leg power).

**Description:** The athlete hops over 10–20 m depending on age and training experience.

**Coaching points:** Encourage a chest and head-up position and flat-footed landings. The hopping leg should be cycled under the body and brought to the front in preparation for each take-off. Landings should be active, with the foot pulled back just before striking the ground to maintain as much forward momentum as possible. This is an advanced technique that requires power and strength. Arms should be coordinated with the legs.

**Do:** 4 x 15–20 m (2 on both legs).

**Variation:** When training older athletes you can add a short run-up, limited to 3–7 strides – this will increase the speed of the drill and require greater landing forces to be overcome. You can also add a jump to the end of the series of hops into a sandpit, and record the distance travelled as a marker of strength, power and technique.

# drill 74 triple jump step

**Objective:** To learn the step phase of the triple jump.

**Description:** The step is performed by jumping from one leg to the other. The athlete starts from a standing position and leaps forward to land flat-footed on their other leg.

**Coaching points:** An elevated chest and head looking forward position must be stressed. The athlete must be encouraged to swing their non-take-off leg forward powerfully at take-off (as with the other jumping drills) and then to hold it for as long as they can before landing on it. Steps should be performed using both legs to ensure even strength development.

**Do:** 6 on each leg.

**Variation:** Perform the step from a short 3- or 5-stride approach.

# drill 75 multiple steps

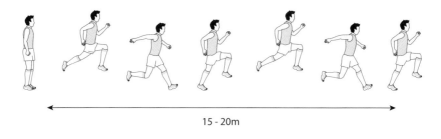

15 - 20m

Hold flight phase

**Objective:** To learn the triple jump step phase and develop leg power for all events.

**Description:** From a standing start the athlete performs a series of steps over 15–20 m (the distance should reflect the age and training maturity of the athletes).

**Coaching points:** Encourage a head-up, looking forward position throughout. As with hopping (*see* Drill 73) the foot should be pulled back just before striking the ground to pull the athlete forward into the next step. This will maintain speed across the steps. Useful coaching phrases: tell the athlete to, 'wait for the ground to come to them' and to 'hold the flight time of each step for as long as they can'.

**Do:** 4 repetitions.

**Variation:** Perform 4–10 steps with a run-up of 5–9 strides (depending on age and training maturity). This is an advanced drill and should only be performed by athletes with the necessary strength, power and technique. Measure the distance achieved to monitor training progression.

# drill 76 standing triple jump

Hop with stronger leg

Hop          Step          Jump

**Objective:** To learn to triple jump at a low intensity.

**Equipment:** Running track or triple jump pit.

**Description:** From a standing position, the athlete hops, steps and jumps.

**Coaching points:** Some athletes may have difficulty coordinating the triple jump movement. A useful phrase to explain how they should move their legs, to perform the 3 phases, is to say, 'same leg, other leg, feet together'. You could also use hoops or draw circles for each landing phase. The distance between them can be increased as the athlete learns the triple jump movement.

As with all the jumps an elevated chest and head-up position should be maintained and the arms should balance the flight phase. Refer to the previous drills for specific coaching points regarding the hops and the step.

**Do:** 6 repetitions.

# *drill 77* short approach triple jump

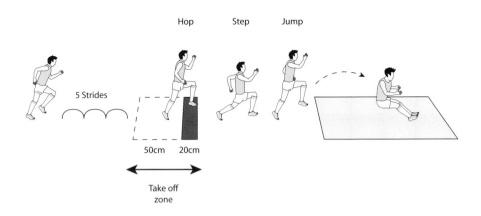

Hop     Step     Jump

5 Strides

50cm    20cm

Take off zone

The great thing about the triple jump is that athletes will display rapid improvements in terms of distances achieved in a just few coaching sessions.

**Objective:** To learn to perform the triple jump from a short run-up with speed.

**Equipment:** Triple jump pit, chalk.

**Description:** Mark a take-off zone next to the triple jump board (*see* Drill 62). Depending on age the athlete should use a 5- to 9-stride run-up. The athlete should start their run-up with the same foot as they will hop from (the first triple jump phase).

**Coaching points:** To encourage balanced jump phases draw lines at relevant points from the triple jump board to the pit to encourage the athlete to travel across these. Initially go for a 4:3:4 ratio. Pay particular attention to the length of the step as this is invariably the phase that is too short. The arms should provide balance during the jump and the torso should be held upright across the phases. Note: It may be necessary to mark a take-off zone at a safe but attainable distance back from the pit, as the official boards may be too far back.

**Do:** 6 jumps.

# HURDLING DRILLS

Hurdling is modified sprinting; it's important to get this across to young athletes – the hurdles should not be jumped, rather they should be skimmed. The event is very rhythmic.

Hurdles are a trip hazard so soft foam hurdles should be used for ages 7–11. When 'proper' hurdles are introduced you must stress that they should only be jumped in the correct way (with the hurdles' legs facing the athlete); failure to do so will result in injuries. Hurdle 'toppling weights' need to be adjusted so that they match the hurdle height setting – contact a qualified hurdles coach or the running track's ground staff to obtain these if you do not know them yourself.

# *drill 78* hurdle walking

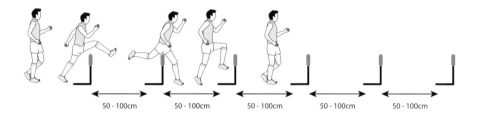

50 - 100cm    50 - 100cm    50 - 100cm    50 - 100cm    50 - 100cm

**Objective:** To develop a feel for the hurdle action and specific flexibility.

**Equipment:** 6–10 hurdles.

**Description:** Space the hurdles approximately 50–100 cm apart (depending on the size and age of the athletes). The lead leg is lifted and pointed at the hurdle, taken over it and pulled down towards the track on the other side, as the other leg (the trail leg) is pulled from behind the body and across the hurdle, in a parallel or near parallel to the ground position. This leg is then pulled through further and rotated to a knee-facing-forward position and placed on the ground in front of the lead leg. The athlete then crosses the remaining hurdles as described.

**Coaching points:** Emphasise an elevated trunk position and try to encourage little twisting of the torso as the athlete cross the hurdles. Do not set the hurdles too high for the athlete to step over.

**Do:** 4 x 6 repetitions (2 with each lead leg).

# drill 79 trail leg drill

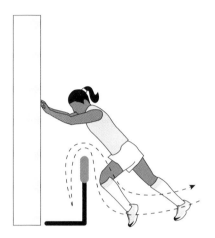

**Objective:** To learn the hurdling trail leg movement.

**Equipment:** Hurdles (foam hurdles to be used for the 7–11 age group) and wall.

**Description:** The athlete faces the wall. They place their hands at shoulder height and lean forwards (they should walk their feet back to achieve this) – their body should be at a 45- to 60-degree angle. Place a hurdle to the right or left of their trail leg. The leg is then lifted back and pulled round, forwards and over the hurdle, in the way that it would cross the hurdle when actually hurdling.

**Coaching points:** Tell the athlete to 'snap' the leg back down to the track as it is pulled over the hurdle. The thigh should be parallel, or near parallel, to the top of the hurdle as it passes over it. The torso should not be overly rotated to allow for the trail leg movement (insufficient specific range of movement may hamper this and will need to be developed if this is the case). Starting with very low hurdles will develop this over time.

**Do:** 10 to each side.

**Variation:** The speed of the drill can be increased once proficiency and range of movement has developed.

# drill 80
## trail leg isolation drill over multiple hurdles

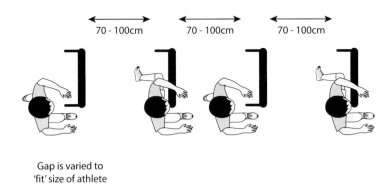

70 - 100cm    70 - 100cm    70 - 100cm

Gap is varied to
'fit' size of athlete

**Objective:** To coach the trail leg hurdle action.

**Equipment:** 6–10 hurdles (foam hurdles to be used for the 7–11 age group).

**Description:** The athlete stands to one side of a row of hurdles – these are spaced approximately 70–100 cm apart, depending on the size of the athlete. They step forward with their lead leg, so that it passes to the side of the hurdle. As they do this they bring their trail leg over and to the front of the hurdle to initiate the trail leg hurdle clearance action. When this leg's foot hits the ground they step forward, again with their lead leg past the next hurdle and bring the trail leg over and to the front again. The drill is repeated until all the hurdles are cleared.

**Coaching points:** Specific hurdling mobility will develop through use of this and other relevant drills. The athlete's torso must be kept as straight on to the front as possible, although there will be some rotation around the hip as the trail leg is lifted, rotated and pulled over the hurdles. Coordinate opposite arm to leg movement, as when sprinting.

**Do:** 6 repetitions.

**Variation:** The drill can be performed at jogging pace, with one or three strides between hurdles (the spacing will need to be adjusted accordingly).

# drill 81 | lead leg isolation drill over multiple hurdles

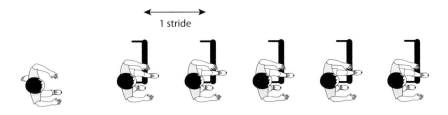

1 stride

Trail leg clears hurdle
Lead leg passes to side of hurdle

**Objective:** To learn the lead leg hurdle movement.

**Equipment:** 6–10 hurdles (foam hurdles can be used for the 7–11 age group).

**Description:** The athlete takes their lead leg over the hurdle. The trail leg passes by the side of the hurdle and does not clear it. The hurdles should be spaced to allow 1 stride to be taken between them.

**Coaching points:** The lead leg should be lifted up towards the hurdle initially bent before being straightened as it passes over the hurdle. It is then pulled down towards the ground and the trail leg pulled past the hurdle.

**Do:** 6 repetitions.

**Variation:** Using a short approach, 1 or 3 strides can be taken between the hurdles. The gap between the hurdles will need to be extended to allow for this.

# drill 82 lead leg/trail leg drill

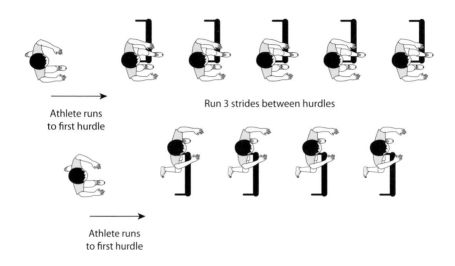

Athlete runs to first hurdle

Run 3 strides between hurdles

Athlete runs to first hurdle

**Objective:** To develop hurdle technique at speed.

**Equipment:** 8–12 hurdles (foam hurdles to be used for the 7–11 age range).

**Description:** Using two lanes on the running track, position the hurdles so they are staggered and separated enough to allow the athlete to 'lead' over one hurdle, run three strides and 'trail' over the next (this drill combines the isolation hurdle movements of the previous two drills).

**Coaching points:** Stress the importance of rhythm and the precise execution of the lead and trail movements.

**Do:** 6 repetitions.

# drill 83 run over 1 hurdle from start

**Objective:** To learn sprint hurdling start.

**Equipment:** Hurdles (foam hurdles to be used for the 7–11 age group).

**Description:** The athlete performs a standing or sprint start (if they are suitably proficient at this – *see* Drill 40), accelerates and clears the hurdle.

**Coaching points:** To clear the hurdle from their preferred leg will require specific foot positioning in the start position. The normal number of strides made to the first hurdle is 7–8 under race conditions, thus if the athlete runs 8 strides to the first hurdle their left foot should be forward in the start position. Adjust the positioning of the hurdle from the start so that the correct number of strides is made. As the young athlete develops maturity and proficiency the hurdle can gradually be moved further away from the start and placed in its correct position.

As the athlete needs to sight the hurdle to clear it, they should be almost upright by their 3rd to 4th stride out from the start.

**Do:** 6 repetitions.

# drill 84 consistent three-stride hurdling

7-8 strides

3 strides

5 hurdles

**Objective:** To start and clear 5 hurdles and develop race pace awareness.

**Equipment:** Hurdles.

**Description:** From a sprint start (*see* Drill 40) the athlete runs 7 or 8 strides to the first hurdle (depending on their age, training and preference), clears it and the next 4 at speed, taking 3 strides between each and adhering to the technical points relating to the lead and trail leg action covered in the previous hurdle drills in this section. The hurdles should be spaced so this can be achieved.

**Coaching points:** Hurdling requires a modified sprint action and the hurdles should be skimmed (not climbed). As with all the drills in this section, moving the hurdles closer together (as opposed to using their official spacings) will encourage this and develop the speed and rhythm required for this event.

**Do:** 6 repetitions.

**Variation:** Set up lanes and add a competitive element. Learning to run one's own race and not get distracted is very important in the hurdles.

# THROWING DRILLS

All the throwing events – the javelin, discus, hammer and shot – have their own specific techniques. These are often not taught as widely as the track and jumping events for a number of reasons, perhaps the most obvious being safety concerns. However, young people enjoy throwing and they are valuable skills that should be encouraged. It is the job of the coach to make this fun and safe. The throwing drills in this section are designed with both these aims in mind. In keeping with the underlying aim of this book, foundation throwing skills will be developed through the drills.

Note: Specific hammer drills are not included, although many of the other throwing drills will be of relevance to this event.

## Throwing event safety

UK Athletics offers health and safety guidelines and risk assessments for all track and field events – *see* page 123 for contact details. Running tracks also have their relevant procedures and assessments. You should always conduct a risk assessment for your coaching session, whatever your location.

One basic piece of advice – no one should ever stand in front of the thrower.

Balls, quoits and turbo javelins can all be safely used to develop throwing skills until the athletes are mature enough to handle shots, discuses, hammers and javelins.

## drill 85 standing football throw

Follow through

**Objective:** To develop basic throwing ability and power.

**Equipment:** Size 4 football (light medicine or jelly ball).

**Description:** Facing the direction of the throw the athlete performs a football-style throw in. Their feet should be parallel and just beyond shoulder-width apart.

**Coaching points:** Arms are kept long and the ball taken back overhead as far as possible within the athlete's flexibility. They should keep their body tall throughout the throwing phase. Encourage a follow-through of a few steps after the ball has been thrown. This will develop the recovery skills needed for the javelin throw, for example, after release.

**Do:** 10 repetitions.

**Variation:** Throw from a split stance position: the athlete takes a big step forward into a lunge position as they throw the ball. This will make it even more javelin specific. Use a light medicine or jelly ball, or shot for 12- to 17-year-olds.

# drill 86 seated overhead football throw

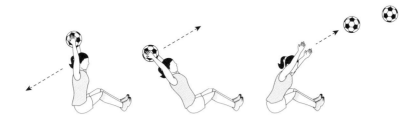

**Objective:** To develop throwing power and awareness of the torso's contribution to throwing.

**Equipment:** Size 4 or 5 football, or light jelly or medicine ball.

**Description:** The athlete sits with their feet just beyond shoulder-width apart, with their knees bent to 90 degrees. They keep their arms long and take the ball back behind their head, taking their torso towards the ground as they do so. They then dynamically bring their body forward to throw the ball whilst keeping their arms long and feet in contact with the ground.

**Coaching points:** Stress the importance of keeping tall throughout the throwing movement and the contribution that the core makes to the throw. The arms should be slightly bent throughout.

**Do:** 10 repetitions.

**Variation:** Measure the throws to introduce an element of competition. 12- to 17-year-olds (with relevant training) can use light medicine balls or jelly balls.

# drill 87 standing backwards, two-handed overhead throw

**Objective:** To develop throwing power and the importance of using the legs when throwing.

**Equipment:** Size 4 or 5 football (or light medicine or jelly ball).

**Description:** The athlete stands with their back to the direction of the throw, their feet significantly wider than shoulder-width apart (to allow the ball to be swung between their legs). The ball is held in two hands and the arms extended overhead. The athlete brings the ball down, keeping their arms long, whilst bending their knees and torso (the ball is taken through the legs). They then swing back up. More than one preliminary swing can be taken. To throw the ball the legs drive dynamically upwards as the ball is taken up. The throw is made just before the arms are at right angles to the ground.

**Coaching points:** Focus the athlete's mind on using their legs – tell them to jump as they throw. They will need to take a few recovery steps after the throw to regain their balance – they should end up facing the direction of the throw.

**Do:** 10 repetitions.

**Variation:** Measure the throws to introduce an element of competition.

standing forwards, two-handed throw

**Objective:** To develop throwing power and the importance of using the legs when throwing.

**Equipment:** Size 4 or 5 football (or light medicine or jelly ball).

**Description:** The athlete faces the direction of the throw, their feet beyond shoulder-width apart (to allow the ball to be swung through them). Their arms are extended and the ball held in both hands to the front of the body and above the head. From this position the ball is brought down quickly whilst bending their legs and torso (the ball is taken through the legs). The athlete then extends their legs dynamically, raises their torso, keeping their arms long and throws the ball.

**Coaching points:** As with the previous drill encourage the athlete to jump forward in time with the throw to really engage their legs. A few recovery steps will need to be taken after the throw to regain balance.

**Do:** 10 throws.

**Variation:** 12- to 16-year-olds (with relevant training) can use light medicine or jelly balls. Again the throw can be measured to add an element of competition.

# drill 89 standing single-arm tennis ball throw

**Objective:** To learn single arm throwing skills relevant to the javelin.

**Equipment:** Tennis ball (or turbo javelin).

**Description:** The athlete stands sideways to the direction of the throw with their feet more than shoulder-width apart. Their front foot faces the direction of the throw, their back foot approximately at right angles to it – the toes of their back foot should be in line with the heel of their front foot. The throwing arm is extended back behind the shoulder and held near to parallel to the ground, palm up. The rear leg is flexed (bent at the knee) and the torso taken back over it, whilst maintaining a side-on position (the athlete should pivot on their rear foot). The other arm is outstretched to the front and held just above parallel to the ground. Leading with the elbow the athlete throws the ball looking in the direction of the throw throughout.

**Coaching points:** It is important to throw over a full range of movement to be javelin-specific and not to 'short arm' throw (throwing it more like a fielder would in cricket).

**Do:** 10 throws.

## drill 90 · turbo javelin throw with three-stride approach

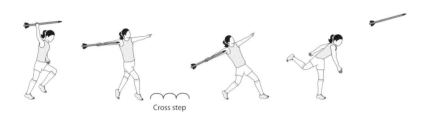

Cross step

**Objective:** To develop javelin throwing technique.

**Equipment:** Turbo javelins.

**Description:** The athlete holds the turbo javelin with their arm extended behind their head. They stand facing the direction of the throw with their feet just wider than shoulder-width apart. For the right-handed thrower the throw should be made on the third stride following a 'left, right, left' sequence. On the penultimate stride a cross step should be taken to advance the athlete's centre of mass in front of the throwing arm and create a backward lean. The javelin is then launched from this position – the throwing stance attained in the previous drill. The body must remain strong and the chest elevated. The athlete will need to perform a recovery stride or two.

**Coaching points:** The arm must remain long until it is brought forward to throw the turbo javelin on the last stride. Encourage the elbow to lead the hand throughout the throw and the hips to be turned into the throw.

**Do:** 10 throws.

**Variation:** Measure the throws to add a competitive element.

turbo javelin carry and cross step

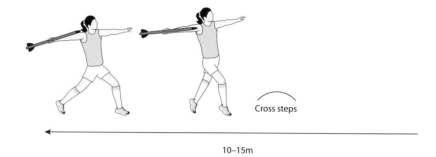

Cross steps

10–15m

**Objective:** To learn the arm carry and cross step action.

**Equipment:** Turbo javelin.

**Description:** The athlete runs over 10–15 m with their throwing arm in the throwing position, i.e. with their arm extended behind their body and palm up, with the non-throwing arm extended in front of them and approximately parallel to the ground. On every other stride they should perform a cross step. This is achieved by taking the same side leg as their throwing arm out to the side with the inside of the thigh advancing – the first stride should be with the cross stepping leg.

**Coaching points:** Encourage a chest facing forward position and ensure that the athlete's arm and turbo javelin remain behind them.

**Do:** 10 throws.

standing quoit throw

**Objective:** To develop basic discus technique.

**Equipment:** Quoit.

**Description:** The athlete faces side-on to the direction of the throw with their feet wider than shoulder-width apart. Their front foot points to the front and the toes of their back foot are lined up with its heel (or slightly behind it). The quoit is held with the palm to the top, fingers outstretched. The athlete performs some preliminary swings. Keeping their arms long the legs flex and rotate in time with the movement. To throw, the athlete pivots on the ball of their back foot, and bends their back leg, their torso should virtually face in the opposite direction of the throw for a split second. As they turn into the throw they straighten their back leg, lifting their torso, before releasing the quoit.

**Coaching points:** The body should lift on release – enabling power to be transferred into the throw from the legs. The chest should remain elevated with the arm following the quoit on release. Encourage a recovery stride.

**Do:** 10 throws.

two-handed football chest pass

Press ball away

**Objective:** To learn the pressing movement associated with the shot put.

**Equipment:** Size 4 football (light medicine ball or jelly ball).

**Description:** The athlete stands tall with their feet shoulder-width apart and holds the ball in two hands to the side and rear of the ball, and in front of and close to their chest. From this position they press the ball away to throw it.

**Coaching points:** Encourage a full extension of the arms on release of the ball and a high chest position.

**Do:** 10 throws.

**Variation:** Step the dominant foot back to open the stance and achieve a lunge position similar to the base of the discus and javelin drills (89 and 92). The athlete should pivot back over this leg whilst bending it and turning their trunk (this should face away from the direction of the throw). They then lift and rotate as they move to the front to press the ball away.

Older and more experienced athletes could throw a medicine or jelly ball.

# drill 94 side-on shot put

Rotates against
direction of throw

Lift and rotate through the
legs, hips and torso into the
direction of the throw

**Objective:** To learn the shot throwing position.

**Equipment:** Tennis ball/light shot/small jelly ball.

**Description:** The athlete faces side-on to the direction of the throw with their feet wider than shoulder-width apart. Their front foot points to the front and the toes of their back foot are lined up with its heel (or slightly behind it). This opens up the stance and allows the hips to rotate into the throw – a vital requirement of all the throwing events. The ball is supported more on the fingers than the palm and nestled against the lower part of the neck. The throwing elbow is held high and the non-throwing arm angled slightly upwards and extended in front of the body. To throw, the athlete pivots on their feet to turn their torso against the direction of the throw, bending their rear leg. They then turn dynamically to the front to throw the ball as their chest elevates. Their throwing arm chases the ball away.

**Coaching points:** Initially emphasise the fluidity of the movement and not the distance thrown. Throwing power comes through the legs and hips and into the arm.

**Do:** 10 throws.

# drill 95 side step and shot action throw

Side step into throwing stance

**Objective:** To learn to throw the shot with increased speed.

**Equipment:** Jelly ball/shot/tennis ball.

**Description:** The athlete stands side-on to the throw with their feet shoulder-width apart. The ball is cradled in the neck and the elbow held up and parallel to the ground. Their other arm is elevated and held almost parallel to the ground, with the hand pointing forwards. Keeping low and driving from the rear leg they move dynamically sideways (to side step) into the throwing stance. They then throw the ball as described in Drill 94.

**Coaching points:** As with the previous drill spend time concentrating on the contribution to the throw made by the legs and hips, rather than worrying about the distance thrown.

**Do:** 10 throws.

# RELAY DRILLS

Relays are a great way to encourage healthy competition and to further develop athletic skills. Shown here are both fun and more serious relay practice drills.

# *drill 96* snake and up-sweep baton pass

'Right'      'Left'      'Right'      'Left'

Up-sweep into hand
Pass on 'whistle'

**Objective:** To learn the up-sweep method of baton changing.

**Equipment:** Batons, whistle.

**Description:** Form teams of 4. In a lane the team jogs forwards and the baton is passed through the team from the back to the front. When the baton reaches the front, the three other runners run to the front, maintaining their order and the drill is repeated. This process continues for a designated number of changeovers or distance. Blow a whistle to indicate when the changes should be made. The baton should go from right hand, to left hand, down the line as this reflects 4 x 100 m requirements. The outgoing runner (baton receiver) takes their arm back and makes a bridge with their thumb and fingers (these face the ground). This will be the target for the incoming runner (baton passer) to 'sweep' the baton up into.

**Coaching points:** All members of the team look straight ahead and not for the baton. Make sure the athletes keep close enough so that the baton can be passed.

**Do:** 4–6 depending on the distance run and the number of changeovers.

**Variation:** Increase the speed of the drill and vary the intervals between blowing your whistle.

snake and down-sweep baton pass
(12- to 16-year-olds)

'Right'          'Left'          'Right'          'Left'

Down-sweep baton pass

**Objective:** To learn the down-sweep method of baton changing.

**Equipment:** Batons, whistle.

**Description:** Set up as per the previous drill. The down-sweep method requires the hand of the outgoing runner to be turned up and fingers spread, so that the baton can be swept down into it. The advantage of this method is that the sprint action does not have to be significantly altered for either athlete involved in the changeover. The baton should be passed from right to left, with the whistle indicating when the changes should be made.

**Coaching points:** The outgoing runner does not look for the baton and only takes their hand back when they hear the whistle.

**Do:** 4–6 depending on the distance run and the number of changeovers.

**Variation:** With practice the changeovers can be made without the whistle. Instead the incoming runner should shout 'hand' when close enough to pass the baton. On hearing this the receiving athlete takes their hand back ready to take the baton. The change is hopefully instantaneous!

# drill 98 — snake and push baton pass (12- to 16-year-olds)

'Right'        'Left'        'Right'        'Left'

Push baton into hand

**Objective:** To learn the push method of baton changing.

**Equipment:** Batons, whistle.

**Description:** Set the drill up as per the previous relay drills. The incoming runner pushes the baton into the hand of the outgoing runner by extending their arm forward as a continuation of the forward arm swing of the sprint arm action. The baton is held at a right angle to the wrist. The outgoing runner's hand is turned up with fingers spread, and their hand is fixed in this position until the baton is received.

**Coaching points:** As for the previous drill.

**Do:** 4–6 depending on the distance run and the number of changeovers.

**Variation:** As for the previous drills.

# pair relay (using up-sweep, down-sweep or push methods)

Athlete 2          Athlete 1

**Objective:** To develop baton changing confidence and technique at speed.

**Equipment:** Batons.

**Description:** Pair the athletes and allocate them to a straight lane on the track. Athlete 1 begins running and athlete 2 a second or so later with a baton. Athlete 2 catches athlete 1 and passes the baton. Athlete 1 slows allowing athlete 2 to take the lead and a further changeover can be made, this time from athlete 1 to athlete 2. The drill is continued like this for a set distance or number of changes.

**Coaching points:** Pair the runners in terms of similar speeds – you don't want to leave a runner stranded with the baton whilst their partner runs out of sight! In terms of the handover method, with 7- to 11-year-olds it will be best to use the up-sweep method (*see* Drill 96), older and more experienced athletes can experiment with all three passing techniques.

**Do:** 4–6 runs depending on length of run and number of baton passes.

# MISCELLANEOUS DRILLS

The drills in this section are designed to give agility, speed and endurance to athletes. They are suitable for all events.

speed bounds

**Objective:** To develop increased leg power – this drill will give a boost to acceleration in particular.

**Description:** From a standing start the athlete pushes themselves forwards using an exaggerated leg drive.

**Coaching points:** Use the phrase 'straight leg running' to get across what the aim of this drill is. There should be a slight forward lean of the trunk as the athlete pushes the ground behind them as dynamically as possible. Speed bounds are a hybrid between multiple steps, also known as bounding (*see* Drill 75), and sprinting.

**Do:** 6 repetitions over 20 m.

**Objective:** To develop fast running and speed endurance.

**Equipment:** Stopwatch and cone.

**Description:** The athlete runs for 30 seconds as fast as they can and the distance they complete is recorded.

**Coaching points:** First timers will probably have no idea how to judge their pace. Under-12s will probably recover relatively quickly afterwards as they have an abundance of energy; older and more experienced athletes will be aware of the nature of the task, will be better able to run at the relevant pace and will probably be more fatigued at the end of it.

As the athlete's fitness and pace judgement improves they will be able to run further in the 30 seconds – this will be a great motivator.

**Do:** 1 run (at the end of a training session).

**Variation:** Increase or decrease the time of the run (from 10–60 seconds).

# USEFUL CONTACTS

## UK Athletics

The governing body for athletics in the UK, UK Athletics runs numerous activities and courses designed to improve athletic performance and coaching skills.

Athletics House,
Central Boulevard,
Blythe Valley Park,
Solihull,
West Midlands B90 8AJ
Tel: 0121 7138 400
www.ukathletics.net
Email: information@ukathletics.org.uk

## Shine Awards

The Norwich Union Shine Awards are an individual award scheme for schools and athletics clubs. There are various running, jumping and throwing activities for athletes aged between 3 and 18.

www.norwichunionshineawards.com
Helpline: 0870 740 7306

## Power of 10

UK Athletics launched Power of 10 in 2006 to transform athletics by 2012. Its aim is to improve every event performance in age groups from under 13 throughout the UK. The Power of 10 is based on a rankings system.

www.powerof10.info

### England Athletics
www.englandathletics.org

### English Schools Athletics Association
www.esaa.net

### Scottish Athletics
www.scottishathletics.org.uk

### Welsh Athletics
www.welshathletics.org

## Sports Coach UK

Sports Coach UK is a charitable organisation and is the lead agency for the development of the UK coaching system – www.sportscoach.co.uk

## Peak Performance

www.pponline.co.uk
Extensive website and newsletter with lots of sports training information.

To find out where your nearest running track is go to: www.runtrackdir.com